MANJU KUMARI SINGH hails from a princely Rajput family in Jaipur. She obtained her Senior Cambridge School Certificate at M.G.D., the first girls' public school in India, and Bachelors Degree, from Maharani's College, Jaipur. She took a keen interest in cooking and home economics as a young girl, and at an early stage participated in cooking both ethnic and exotic foods.

Through her travel and stay in several countries, Manju Kumari Singh kept her interest in cooking and developed simple recipes involving local foods, when they lived in Indonesia, Nigeria, England, Switzerland and U.S.A.

She is the author of two popular cook books, "The Spice Box", published by Crossing Press, USA, and "Royal Indian Cookery", published by Marshall Cavendish, England. She has also contributed recipes in newspapers and magazines in India and USA. She has also demonstrated on local television in Washington DC, recipes with emphasis on health food.

SHAAKAHAARI
Indian Vegetarian Cookery

Manju Kumari Singh

HarperCollins *Publishers* India

*Dedicated to
my teacher
Mrs. Mira Varma
who always appreciated and
encouraged me.*

HarperCollins *Publishers* India Pvt. Ltd.
7/16 Ansari Road, Daryaganj, New Delhi 110 002

Published 1996 by HarperCollins Publishers India

© Manju Kumari Singh 1996

Manju Kumari Singh asserts the moral right
to be identified as the author of this work.

ISBN 81-7223-226-8

Design: Supriya Sharma • Typeset at Design on You

All rights reserved.
No part of this publication may be reproduced,
stored in a retrieval system, or transmitted, in any form or by any means,
electronic or mechanical, photocopying, recording or otherwise,
without the prior permission of the publishers.

Printed in India at
Gopsons Papers Ltd.
A 28 Sector IX, NOIDA 201 301

Contents

- 9 Introduction
- 11 Spice & Herbs Index
- 21 Useful Basic Recipes for Indian Cookery
- 26 Basic Indian Implements
- 27 Weights & Measures

31 Aperitifs & Drinks
- 33 Jal Jeera
- Meethi Lassi Dilkush
- 34 Namkeen Lassi
- Gajjar Kaanji
- 35 Tamatar ka Ras
- Nimboo Shikanji
- 36 Nimboo ka Sherbat
- Imli ka Soda Paani
- 37 Aam ka Panna
- Amras
- 38 Kharbooze ka Panna
- Ananaas ka Sherbet
- 39 Masala Milk Shake
- Badaam ka Doodh
- 40 Ande ka Doodh
- Kele ka Doodh
- 41 Thandai
- 42 Thandi Chai
- Elaichi ki Chai
- 43 Thandi Coffee

45 Naashte ke Pakwaan
- 47 Saade Pakore
- Cheese ke Bhajiye
- 48 Methi Pakore
- 49 Aloo Matar Samosa
- 50 Dal ki Kachori
- 51 Dhokla
- Dahi Bhalla
- 53 Aaloo ki Tikki
- 54 Bhel Puri
- 55 Dahi Papri Chaat
- 56 Aaloo Chaat
- Phalon ki Chaat
- 57 Masala Dosai
- 58 Idli
- 59 Madrasi Vadai
- Mung Phalli ka Upma
- 60 Chaklis
- 61 Matthi
- Aaloo aur Roti ka Upma
- 62 Chaawal aur Aaloo Roll
- 63 Khandwi Rolls
- 64 Bhutte aur Aaloo ke Cutlets
- 65 Baigan ke Cutlets
- 66 Bhutte ka Toast
- Aaloo ke Kebab
- 67 Dahi Toast
- Cheese Straws
- 68 Namkeen Kaaju
- Pyaaz ke Bhajiye

69 Shorbe
- 71 Matar ka Shorba
- Aaloo ke Shorba
- 72 Chaawal ka Shorba
- Tamatar aur Kothmir Rasam
- 73 Pyaaz ka Shorba
- 74 Gobhi ka Shorba

Contents

75 Ande ke Pakwaan
77 Bharwa Ande
78 Ande aur Gobhi ke Pakore
   Katori ke Ande
79 Sunheri Ande
80 Angrezi Anda Galantine
   Ande ki Ankuri
81 Desi Omelette
82 Ande ki Biryani
83 Bharwa Ande ke Pyaaz
84 Ande aur Paalak ka Saalan
85 Anda Mattar Curry
86 Ande ke Kofte
87 Katori ke Ande

89 Tarkaariyan
91 Aloo ka Saag
92 Karahi wale Aaloo
93 Aloo Haryali
94 Dibbe ki Sabzi
95 Paalak Paneer Kofta Curry
96 Subz Kebab
97 Paneer ka Soola
98 Mattar Paneer
99 Dhingri Mattar
100 Pudina Baigan
101 Mirch ka Saala
102 Baiganmka Bharta
103 Meethe Tamatar
    Kola ka Saag
104 Sabut Bhindi
105 Khatte Chole
106 Tawa Chana

107 Achaari Gobhi
    Kaande ka Saag
108 Punjabi Karhi
109 Sindhi Karhi

111 Dal ke Pakwaan
114 Subzi Waali Dal
115 Sambhar
116 Tuwar Dal Tarke Waali
117 Meethi Gujrati Dal
118 Malka Masoor Matar Waali
119 Mung Dal Malai Waali
120 Dal Haryali
121 Rajasthani Gaadi Dal with
    Khaand
122 Chana Dal Lauki Waali
123 Dal Makhani
124 Punjabi Maah Sabat

125 Bhaartiya Rotis
127 Phulka
128 Chappatis
129 Puris
130 Tandoori Roti
131 Tawa Paranthas
132 Bharwa Paneer Paranthas
133 Batia
134 Baati
135 Khurmi Naan
136 Podhina Bhatura

137 Chaawal ke Pakwaan
139 Saade Chaawal

Contents

    Khichree
140 Makhani Chaawal
    Matar Pullao
141 Gatte ka Pullao
142 Baigaan ka Pullao
143 Paneer Pullao
144 Methi ke Chaawal
145 Sabut Masoor ki Biryani
146 Katori ka Chaawal
147 Bisi Bele Huliyanna
148 Tirange Chaawal

149 Raitas
151 Dahi ki Chatni
    Lauki ka Raita
152 Arbi ka Raita
    Chane aur Aaloo ka Raita
153 Dubble Roti ka Raita
    Anannas ka Raita
154 Mooli ka Raita
    Matar ka Raita
155 Ankur ka Raita
156 Karam Khalle ka Raita

157 Chutneys
159 Dhania ki Chutney
    Pudhine ki Chutney
160 Lassan Chutney
    Tamatar ki Chutney
161 Churri Chutney
    Lal Mirchi ki Chutney
162 Khopre ki Chutney
    Dosa Chutney

163 Hare Aam ki Chutney
    Imli aur Adrak ki Sonth
164 Simla Mirch ki Chutney
165 Kairee ki Meethi Chutney
166 Seb ki Chutney

167 Achaar
169 Hari Mirch ka Achaar
170 Meetha Neembu ka Achaar
    Nimboo Masala Achaar
171 Mirchi Walla Aam ka Achaar
172 Pyaaz ka Achaar
173 Ande ka Achaar
    Amrud ki Cheese
174 Papita ka Achaar

175 Meethe Pakwaan
177 Badaam ka Halwa
178 Gajjar ka Halwa
179 Chana ki Dal ka Halwa
180 Mung ki Dal ka Halwa
181 Matar ki Barfi
182 Aam ki Barfi
183 Aaloo ki Barfi
184 Khopre ki Barfi
185 Gulab Jamun
186 Naariyal aur Chocolate ke Laddu
    Churma Laddu
187 Khoa ki Gujiya
188 Elaichi Kheer

189 Samaapt
191 Glossary

Introduction

'Shaakahaari' literally means vegetarian. Indian cookery has a homogeneous tradition and varies from coast to coast and is based on a complex fusion of different cultures, castes and regions.

'Indian vegetarian curry fever' has spread all over the world. It is a trend in this day and age to become a vegetarian. Normally natural foods are vegetarian. I have written several books on Indian cuisine and cookery over the years and gradually getting addicted to vegetarian cookery. Old wives tales go on to say that a vegetarian lives a longer life! Fresh vegetables are good for digestion and are nutritious. Frozen foods are not included in our Indian cooking. We believe in eating fresh vegetables and fresh fruits. Many Indians shop daily for fresh vegetables. Street vendors sell vegetables and fruits of the season, on flat wooden carts and go peddling from door to door and street to street.

Spices play a major role in Indian cookery. Some spices are freshly ground, roasted and powdered daily, to get the authentic aroma and flavour in the curries.

In a vegetarian Indian kitchen no shoes are allowed. Food is prepared after having a bath. The kitchen is considered a sacred place. In India food is generally served in a 'thaali' (a round platter with small cups called 'katoris' placed around). In the south people prefer to eat on fresh clean banana leaves. The traditional Indian way is to eat Japanese style! i.e. to sit on the floor and put the food platter on a low stool in front.

India is such a vast country, the food habits are mostly geographical and climatic. The northern part mainly eats wheat, e.g. chappatis, thrice a day, while rice is eaten in the south, east and coastal towns of India. The contribution of the British Raj was the loaf of bread which is called 'Dubble Roti' because I think it rises very high after baking, a contrast to the flat leavened Indian 'chappati'! It is generally eaten for breakfast or as ordinary or toasted sandwiches.

Cooking is a traditional institution in every Indian home. Food is ceremoniously prepared with great pride and joy and is the nucleus of the daily household activity.

In the Hindu religion only vegetarian food is strictly eaten. No life was slain and only vegetarian food was prepared in the very orthodox Hindu homes. With the advent of the Muslims and other conquerors, India went through a radical change in its eating habits. Exotic dishes were introduced by the Mughal and Persian conquerors while British fare was introduced in affluent homes.

Indian vegetarian cuisine is perhaps the world's greatest vegetarian cuisine with so much variation and variety to suit every palate. Always remember that Indian cooking is very flexible and can be adapted to one's taste and suitability. There is a great growing interest in Indian vegetarian cooking. I would like to share some of my favourite vegetarian recipes with the vegetarians of the world!

My recipes are very simplified and easy to follow. Every vegetable can be curried by all Indians!

People have become very health conscious and 'Shaakahaarism' (vegetarianism) is spreading all over the diet-conscious people of the world.

Happy 'Shaakahaari' currying to you all.

Yours vegetarianly,

Manju Kumari Singh

Spice and Herb Index

Spices and Herbs play a major role in Indian culinary cuisine. It gives the cuisine its distinctive and aromatic flavor. They also aid in digestion and make the food tastier and more palatable.

Most spices are grown and reach their maturity in moist, sunny tropical climates. India grows a lot of its spices, e.g. chillies, coriander, cumin, cardamoms, fenugreek, ginger, pepper, sesame, turmeric, mustard etc.

Many spices can be obtained at health food stores, supermarkets or Indian specialist grocery stores in the suburbs of a big city. One can also order them in small amounts by mail through the specialist shops. They can be then frozen in thick or double plastic bags to retain their freshness and also avoid insect attack!

One must try and remember the Indian spice names, as it helps in buying the spices and knowing your spices from one another. One must try and get familiar with each ingredient in order to enjoy and savour the culinary delights of Indian vegetarian cookery.

Listed below are some of the important and most avidly used spices and herbs, with English, Latin and Indian names.

ANISEED
Pimpinella Anisum—Sounf

This plant belongs to the parsley family. The tiny minute seeds are called aniseed and they resemble the shape and size of a cumin seed. They are liquorice flavoured seeds, used in pickles, snacks, chutneys etc. They also aid digestion and are boiled in water to soothe a newly born baby's fragile stomach! Aniseeds are roasted and eaten after every curry meal to aid digestion.

ASAFOETIDA
Heeng

This is a hard resin which has a very pungent aroma. It is sold in powdered form these days in tiny plastic boxes. Just a pinch of 'heeng' is added to vegetable curries or 'dals' (lentils). It has an annoying penetrating smell which can be smelt miles away! Always close the kitchen and put on the exhaust fan while using this ingredient. It has a digestive effect. A 'heeng baghaar' is always used when cooking certain vegetables and lentils.

BAY LEAF
Tej Patta

The bay leaf comes from the cassia tree. The leaf has the same flavour as cinnamon. Bay leaf is used in a 'baghaar' (seasoning). The leaves are mostly used in rice dishes and should not be eaten, they only flavour the dish.

BLACK PEPPER
Piper Nigrum—Kaali Mirch

Black pepper is a product of the tropics. It is the world's most important spice. Pepper is produced from a climbing vine which is grown in the East Indies and India. It is a perennial climber, which grows in damp tropical jungles. Black pepper is a remedy for sore throats. In our home, we drink hot milk flavoured with powdered black pepper, saffron and sugar to chase away a nasty cold and cough! It can be bought in a powdered form or in the form of pepper corns. For best results always use a pepper mill to get that fresh flavour.

BLACK SALT
Kaala Namak

Black salt is a pungent smelling salt. It is used in a particular 'chaat masala' powder, which is commercially sold and can also be made at home. It has a digestive attribute.

CARDAMOM
Ellettaria Cardamomum—Elaichi

There are two different types of cardamoms used in Indian cooking. They are sold in two different colours and sizes and are commonly known as 'badi elaichi'—the big black pod and the 'choti elaichi'—the small oval pale green pod.

Cardamoms are grown in south India and Sri Lanka. The green and black capsule like pods contain about twenty black seeds. These seeds are also used in flavouring sweets and are crushed into a powder. Cardamom powder is one of the ingredients of 'garam masala' powder and is also used in desserts. The small green pods are expensive, so a lot of people use the cheaper big black pods called 'dodaas'. The whole pods are used in flavouring rice or some specific curries. The type of cardamom to be used is indicated in all recipes.

CAROM SEEDS
Ajwain

Carom seeds have digestive property. They are used in flavouring vegetables, e.g., potatoes, coco-yams, etc. and also in snacks and Indian breads. It has a similar flavour like cumin seeds. Carom seeds if boiled in water, aid and soothe a Delhi-belly. When buying it in specialist Indian grocery shops, it is advisable to use its original name.

CHILLIES (GREEN)
Hari Mirch

Green chillies are a source of Vitamin C. In India, we love to use them in snacks and vegetable preparations. Green chillies are used in fresh salads daily along with a pinch of salt and a squeeze of lemon on top. I always use gloves when cutting them, as they easily irritate the sensitive skin of the palms! These are available at most grocery stores. No Indian meal is complete without a green chillie!

CHILLIES (RED)
Capsicum Frutescens— Laal Mirch

They are grown in most places around the world and are a favourite ingredient in India, China, Mexico, South America, Italy and West Indies! The mature fruits are dried in the sun in a large concrete open field. They are used as a dry or fresh condiment in India and can be bought in various sizes. They are dried and then powdered. They can also be coarsely ground in a coffee grinder and then used in various kinds of vegetables, lentils and chutneys.

They can also be soaked in vinegar or water and ground into a thick paste to make vindaloo curries. Many people in Indian villages often eat the chilli paste laced with salt and garlic along with their thick 'rotis' or 'chappatis' daily. It is also my favourite meal. Sherry peppers are also made with dried red chillies soaked in sherry or gin.

CINNAMON
Cinnamomum Zeylanicum—Daal Cheeni

Cinnamon originated in Sri Lanka but is also grown in South India. Cinnamon sticks are a popular spice in our Indian cuisine. These are long, thin, dried quills of a young bark of the cassia tree. They can be used as a whole spice, or used in a powdered form. Cinnamon can be used in making rice 'pullaos' and is an important spice in the 'garam masala' mixture.

CLOVES
Eugenia Aromatica—Laung

Cloves are an aromatic pungent spice ingredient. They are grown in coastal areas on trees growing in loamy soils. The clove buds are harvested before opening and are dried in the sun.

Cloves can be used whole, powdered or as a clove oil. Clove oil aids and soothes a toothache while the whole clove aids in soothing a sore throat, if chewed slowly! Cloves are highly medicinal and antiseptic.

Whole cloves are used in a 'garam masala' mixture. Cloves are used in flavouring rice 'pullaos', vegetables and curries.

CITRIC ACID
Neemboo ka sat

This is a powder which is made from dried lemons. It is a tart and tangy powder used in making savoury mixes and 'chaats'. It is used in making 'chiwra' or seasoning certain vegetables.

COCONUT
Naariyal

Coconut is grown and used in the coastal regions of India. It is used in vegetables, lentils, rice and desserts. It is a very versatile item and can be used fresh, dried, powdered or as a liquid called 'coconut milk'. It gives a fresh flavour to curries. It is also used as an important ingredient in fresh chutneys. Coconut is very auspicious and is offered to our Gods in Hindu temples or as a customary gift to a bride or bridegroom. Coconut oil is also very popular and healthy for the hair.

CORIANDER
Coriandrum Sativum—Dhania

Coriander can be easily grown in a

kitchen garden in a box. Coriander can be used in seed form, or in its powdered form or as fresh coriander leaves. The leaves are also called Chinese parsley or cilentro or in our Hindi language as 'hara dhaniya' or 'kotmil'. It adds flavour to any vegetable, dal or chutney. It is often used as a garnish on curries or rice dishes.

Coriander power is a thickening agent in curries and its seeds are used in some vegetables and snacks. Coriander in any form is available in most grocery stores. It originated in the Middle East and was grown in the Hanging Gardens of Babylon! I always grow my own coriander in a wooden box. When it is ready to cut, I wash it and freeze it in a plastic bag. I just sprinkle a little bit of frozen coriander leaves into a vegetable or lentil dal and it gives it a lovely fresh aromatic and distinctive flavour.

CUMIN
Cuminum Cyminum—
Zeera or Jeera

Cumin is a highly aromatic spice. It is a native of the Middle East. It looks a bit like anise and caraway. It is either used whole or in powdered form in Indian vegetable curries and dals (lentils), or as roasted and then powdered, in yogurt (raitas) and some specific vegetarian dishes and pickles. It is the most avidly used spice in seasoning vegetables, rice, dals, snacks, pickles, breads, chutneys, 'raitas', etc. It aids in digestion if roasted and added to yogurt shakes—'lassi'. There are two types of cumin which we use in India—'kaala zeera' (black cumin) or 'safed zeera' (white cumin). The white cumin is the cheaper one and is used in daily cooking while the black 'zeera' is only used in making special rice, 'pullaos' etc. It looks like caraway seeds but has a totally different flavour. It is also mixed in the 'garam masala' mixture.

Always pick and clean your 'zeera' before using it as it is always full of insects and foreign matter! It is advisable to freeze it if one has more than half a cup of cumin seeds. They stay fresh and free from insect attack!

CURRY LEAVES
Kari Patta

It has a fresh and lingering aroma and is used in all dishes in south Indian cooking and in seasoning vegetables, chutneys, dals, rice, snacks etc. It can be dried in the sun for a week and then stored in air tight jars or frozen fresh in the freezer. Curry leaves are sold commercially in the dried form, unless you shop in India or in an Indian suburb, where it is sold fresh. The tree is found in India, Pakistan and Sri Lanka, but can be grown in any tropical country.

FENNEL
Sounf

It is also called 'fennel' or 'aniseed'. There is always an argument to its being called fennel seed. There are two types of fennel seeds, large and small. The smaller ones are a specialty from a city called Lucknow—the former name of this city during the Raj was Oudh. One always asks for 'Lucknowi Sounf' in a shop. It is avidly eaten raw or roasted and is very sweet. It aids in digestion and is also eaten inside a betel leaf—the famous 'paan'—along with other ingredients as a mouth cleansing after heavy garlic flavoured curry!

FENUGREEK
Trigonella Foenum-graecum—Maithi

Fenugreek is a bitter spice. It belongs to the pea family and is a leguminous plant. It is grown in India, S. Europe, West Asia and North Africa. Fenugreek seeds are used in a 'baghaar' (seasoning) to flavour dals and vegetables. They are used roasted and powdered in pickles and chutneys. They have a penetrating pungent smell. Fenugreek tea is given to young mothers daily, early in the morning for forty days to throw out all the impurities from the abdomen! They are rich in vitamins and protein. In America, it is used in flavouring Maple syrup.

Fresh fenugreek leaves are used in a salad or used with potatoes to make an excellent dry vegetable curry. In Rajasthan, an excellent curry is made solely of raw fresh fenugreek seeds and it tastes like a pea curry. Dried fenugreek leaves are commercially sold in packets and are good in flavouring 'karhi'—a chickpea flour and yogurt soup.

Garam Masala

The word 'garam' means hot and 'masala' means spice so when you join the two words together it becomes hot spice! It is a spice blend which mostly contains 4 teaspoons each of cumin, black pepper corn, cloves, green cardamoms, black cardamoms, cinnamon sticks, black cumin and coriander seeds. This mixture should be stored in a jar. Whenever one needs to use 'garam masala' powder, just grind about a table spoon of this mixture in a coffee grinder for a fresh aromatic flavour. It is a hot subtle spice. The powdered form is always added to a curry at the end, just before the dish is being served. It is used extensively in North Indian cooking. It is very different from curry powder and is sold in packets or air tight tin boxes in grocery shops in the powdered form.

GARLIC
Lahsun

Garlic has many attributes besides being smelly! Always use rubber gloves while peeling garlic, to avoid a permanent stink in your fingertips! Garlic is sold as a whole dried bulb. In India, we buy it in kilos and store it when it is sold cheap. It stores well in a dry climate. It also has medicinal value and is recommended in a diet in order to have a healthy flow of blood.

Garlic can be peeled, chopped and then frozen in a double plastic bag. Garlic is sold in a dehydrated flake form and now also in a garlic puree tube. Indians and Italians swear by this spice and cannot cook many main dishes without garlic. Always remember never to eat garlic on your honeymoon!

GINGER
Zingiber Officinale—Adrak & Sonth

'Adrak' is fresh ginger root while 'Sonth' is the dried form. It originated in South Asia and was first cultivated in India and China. It is now grown in all tropical countries. It is an underground plant with thick, knobby rhizomes which are called ginger root. It is peeled and scraped and washed well before chopping, grating or grinding into a paste. The ginger root is peeled and dried in the sun and then powdered. This powder is sold in most grocery shops. Chinese and Indian cooking use a lot of ginger root cut into thin slices.

It is used in curries, sauces, dals, chutneys, pickles, drinks, and snacks. It has a hot, rich, flavour. Can be bought in a ginger-root form at the green grocers. Left over rhizomes can be placed in a small pot for further use. They will multiply and produce more small ginger-roots.

GHEE
Clarified Butter

'Ghee' is clarified butter. It was the most ancient fat medium used in India. Pure 'ghee' was made at home.

Most households had a small dairy. With modernization this fad has died a natural death and one can now buy commercial 'ghee' in tins. Holland and India produce good 'ghee' for export. In India, we still prefer our hot chappatis buttered with ghee! It is high in cholesterol, so most people with obesity, diabetics, and heart problems avoid it. It is said in some history books that 'ghee' was excavated in some of the old clay pots dug out from the famous 'Harappa' and 'Mohenjodaro' civilizations from the B. C. century and was still not rancid!

JAGGERY
Gur

Molasses, called 'gur', is a brown solidified lump of sweetness sold in kilos. It is made into large one, half or quarter kilo rounds and sold. It can be bought at specialist Indian shops. 'Gur' or jaggery is used in vegetables, desserts, dals, chutneys, pickles, etc. A poor man's treat is a thick 'roti' with a chunk of 'ghee' and a rock or lump of 'gur'! It is cheaper than sugar. It is an auspicious item as when a child is born to a family, 'gur' is distributed to friends and relatives.

LEMON
Neembu

Lemon is a member of the citrus family. It is a very important item in Indian cooking. Lemon juice is used in drinks, vegetables, dals, chutneys and many other dishes. I always squeeze a few lemons and keep the lemon juice in a bottle in the fridge, so it is always there whenever I need it! A refreshing drink in the hot scorching summer is called 'neembu paani'—it can be called thirst aid as it prevents sunstroke and dehydration.

MACE & NUTMEG
Myristica Fragrans—Javitri and Jaiphal

This twin spice is derived from the same fruit. When the fruit ripens it bursts open revealing a dark nut inside called nutmeg. It is encased inside a red woven case called Mace. This wispy mace flat blades, are dried and sold in shops. These are expensive spices and are mostly used sparingly in desserts or in authentic Mughal curries. Nutmeg tastes best in any dish when it is grated as the fresh flavour is obtained.

MANGO POWDER
Amchoor

Mango powder is made from raw mangoes. Green small mangoes are peeled and then sliced and dried in the hot sun for several days until they become leathery. They can be used as dried slices or in a powdered form. They have a tangy flavour. For best results, always soak them in warm water before using them to flavour dals or vegetables. The 'amchoor' powder is sold in tins or packets and is a good substitute for lemon or vinegar.

MINT
Pudina

Mint is a refreshing herb used mainly as a garnish or in fresh ground chutney, breads, curries, etc. Dried mint is used in flavouring yogurt (raitas). Mint grows like a weed in any garden if proper care is taken. It does well in a tropical climate.

MUSTARD SEED
Brassica Nigra—Rai or Sarson

Mustard seeds can be divided into three types—black, yellow or white (alba, Brassica hirta). The black seeds are used in 'baghaar' or 'tarka' (seasoning) in a dal or vegetable. The yellow ones are used by grinding them into a paste and then using in curries. The mustard seeds are usually crushed and mixed in pickles. They have a bitter, sour taste.

Mustard oil is made from mustard seeds. In north eastern parts of India, it is used a lot in cooking vegetables and pickles. It has a penetrating smell. Many people use it for an oil massage for body and hair before a bath! Fresh mustard leaves are eaten in the winter as a green vegetable as a twin combination of 'sarson ka saag' and 'makka ki roti' (corn bread).

NIGELLA OR ONION SEEDS
Kalonji or Mangrail

The nigella seed are deep black in colour and are vastly used in pickles and 'tandoori' dishes and also to garnish the famous unleavened bread—'naan'. They are one of the 'panch foran' ingredients used for a 'baghaar' (seasoning).

POMEGRANATE SEEDS
Anaar daana

These seeds are the dried seeds of the ruby red pomegranate fruit. They are shelled and taken out of the fruit and dried in the sun until they turn black in colour. They are a sour agent and are used in making snacks, chutneys, and yogurt. They must always be washed before use in order to dispel the crunchy muddy flavour!

POPPY SEEDS
Papaver Somniferum—Khus Khus

Poppy seeds are tiny cream coloured round seeds of the Indian opium poppy flower. They have a nutty flavour and are used as a thickening agent in curry sauces. They are mostly roasted on a dry griddle before grinding them in a coffee grinder.

The opium poppy is a native of Asia. Poppy seeds are mostly used in a curry when it is being cooked for a party as it has a rich creamy texture and taste. It is also good in some desserts and sweets.

PAPPADUMS
Papad

Pappadums are paper thin discs made of lentil or rice flour. They are made and dried in the sun. They are salty and spicy and have a preservative. They are then packaged or put into a cellophane wrapper and sealed into a tin box. A lot of companies market them. Most women in North West regions of India—in the State of Gujarat—make their own pappadums monthly, for the family consumption.

As pappadums are raw, they are always deep fried in hot oil. They double in size so be quick to fry one at a time, and drain them out at once with a pair of kitchen tongs onto a paper towel. Some poppadums made from lentils can be roasted dry, on a naked gas flame, by quickly toasting it over the flame and turning it over at once. Rice pappadums are always deep fried. It is a good idea to break them into half before frying, for best results. They are an accompaniment to a curry meal, before or after a meal.

An old Rajasthani tradition in the olden days was that when the food was finished in the kitchen, pappadums were served, thus the guests got a hint that there was no more food in the kitchen. This was practised at large wedding feasts!

Many people eat them after meals as a digestive. In most restaurants around the world, pappadums are served complimentary with your drinks order. For best results, toast a pappadum folded in half inside a toaster oven, or a microwave for 30 seconds on each side on a paper towel.

ROCK SALT
Saindha Namak

It is used in fasting when ordinary salt is not allowed to be eaten on fasting day. It has a distinctive flavour and has the presence of iron salt in it. It can be bought at specialist grocery stores in a rock form. It is crushed into tiny fragments before use, with a mortar and pestle.

SAFFRON
Crocus sativus—Zaffraan or Kesar

This is the world's most expensive spice. It is grown in Kashmir (India), Spain, Portugal and the Middle East. The crop is harvested when the flowers open. Each flower has three flame red funnel-like stigmas. The stigmas are hand-picked and dried. The thread-like strands are carefully packed in boxes and sold in shops. They are weighed in grams.

Saffron is used in exotic Indian desserts or the famous rice 'biryanis'. It is soaked in either hot milk or hot water for best results. It is said that Cleopatra used it as a cosmetic in her days! It has a sweet aromatic pleasing smell and enhances every dish. It is also a colouring agent and dyes the food into a deep golden orange colour.

SESAME SEEDS
Sesamum indicum—Til or Gingilly

This is a native plant of Indonesia and Africa. It is extensively used in India and the Middle East. It is made famous in the story of Ali Baba, when he uttered the words 'Open Sesame' a code word which enables the heavy cave door to open and reveal the treasure trove. The sesame seeds are flat oval shaped seeds in white and brown colour. In India, we roast and grind them into a thick paste to add to curries. They act as a thickening agent and taste like a substitute for peanuts.

Sesame seeds are used in desserts, chutneys, pickles, vegetables and to season rice. Sesame (til) oil is used in India to cook vegetables or in salads. Sesame oil is good for a skin massage also.

TAMARIND
Tamarindus indica—Imli

Tamarind is a leguminous tree which grows in abundance in India, West Indies, East Africa and the Tropics. The tamarind fruit is a seed pod, light brown in colour. The seeds are removed from the pods and it forms into a sticky dark coloured pulp. The pulp contains tartaric acid, which gives the tangy sour taste to the tamarind. The tamarind pulp has a mild laxative property.

Tamarind is used in making chutneys for snacks or to flavour dals and a few vegetables. It can be bought in specialist shops.

TURMERIC
Curcuma longa—Haldi

Turmeric belongs to the ginger family. It is a root rhizome and a vegetable dye. It is used as a spice and a colourant. It is of a bright yellow hue. Turmeric roots are washed and dried in the sun then peeled and made into a fine powder called 'Haldi'. Turmeric is also a medicinal condiment as it treats some ailments like fungus and ulcers etc. In the Eastern world, the ladies rub turmeric paste on their bodies to clean the tan.

Turmeric gives the yellow colour to curries, rice. Turmeric powder is an essential part of the curry powder. Turmeric is never used in sweets, it can be only used in savoury dishes. It is available in most grocery stores in packets or tins.

VINEGAR
Sirka

Dark brown malt vinegar is used in Indian cooking. Vinegar is used in making salads and a few vegetables. In India malt vinegar is also used in rinsing and washing hair. It gives it a glow and shine.

Useful Basic Recipes for Indian Cookery

Indian cooking requires a basic knowledge of the spices, herb and, ingredients. It is always better to know the spice names in the Indian language and to get to recognise them. Before trying out any recipes from this book, it is advisable to know these basic procedures.

AATAA
Whole wheat flour dough

'Aataa' dough is made from whole wheat flour in India. 'Aataa' is made from wheat. It is sold either as whole wheat flour in bags or you have to get your own 'aataa' ground from the flour mill. 'Aataa' is sieved before use in a bowl, a pinch of salt is added and then gradually water is added to make a stiff dough. Keep the dough covered with a damp cloth. Always make the 'aataa' dough ready at least half an hour before use. Knead it well. Left over 'aataa' can be stored in the fridge for the next day in a tupperware box. 'Aataa' is used in making chappatis, paranthas and puris.

BAGHAAR OR TARKA
Oil Seasoning

'Baghaar' or 'Tarka' is given to nearly all Indian curries, dals, chutneys and rice. It is either used at the beginning of the preparation, and in some cases after the dish is cooked. The 'baghaar' procedure for each dish is stated in every recipe.

For a 'baghaar', some oil or ghee is heated in a saucepan for about ten seconds. Then either a teaspoon of cumin or mustard seeds are added along with some chopped garlic or small dried red peppers or curry leaves or even a teaspoon of 'garam masala' mixture, depending upon the ingredients required. This 'baghaar' is either poured over the prepared dish or in some cases of vegetables, the vegetables are added to the pan, after the 'baghaar'; the whole procedure only takes about a minute. Always keep a splatter guard lid ready to cover as soon as anything is dropped into the hot oil, for your own protection.

BESAN GHOL
Chickpea flour batter

'Besan' is the flour of chickpeas, which is sold commercially in all specialist shops. It is an important item in the Indian kitchen as most snacks are made from 'besan'. Always store it in the fridge in a tupperware box. Always seive it before use. It is susceptible to insect attack. It is high in protein and less glutinous. Pea flour can be substituted for 'besan'. And in many cases, substitute it by ordinary white flour after treating it in the way described.

Tie two cups of white flour in a piece of muslin cloth or cheese cloth and steam it in a pan of water for about half an hour. Be careful when pouring water into the steamer pan, the flour should not get wet. Cover and steam. This process takes the gluten out from the flour. Now you can treat it like 'besan' and add about a teaspoon of turmeric to the flour, so that it resembles the pale yellow colour of 'besan'!

BHUNA MASALA
Roasted spices

Some spices are roasted for certain recipes. The most popular one is the cumin. Always clean it before use. Take about 4 tablespoons of cumin seeds and roast them in a dry griddle or pan with no oil. Shake them for a minute and when all are roasted to a dark brown colour, cool them on a plate and then store them in a bottle. You can either keep them whole or powder them in a coffee grinder after cooking them. It is always handy to keep roasted cumin in the kitchen so it is there whenever you are making 'raitas', salads or 'lassi'.

Fenugreek seeds, dried chillies, sesame seeds, poppy and coriander seeds are also roasted in the same way.

CHAACH
Buttermilk

'Chaach' is often consumed during the hot sunny months of May and June in India. Everyone drinks 'chaach' daily with their lunch in the summer to avoid sunstroke. 'Chaach' can be made in the blender by diluting one cup of natural yogurt in 3 to 4 cups of cold water. Blend it and add salt. For digestive purposes a teaspoon of roasted cumin seed powder may be added.

DAHI
Natural yogurt

Yogurt is called 'Dahi' in Hindi. It is used in cooking, marinating and as yogurt salads. 'Dahi' is also called curds in India. One makes 'dahi' daily in the Indian kitchen at night. Warm 4 cups milk to body temperature. Pour into a glass bowl, add 1 tablespoon of yogurt into the milk and stir well. Cover the bowl and place it inside the oven (cool oven). It is ready the next morning after about 10 hours. Take it out and keep it in the fridge. For best results, make milk with milk powder. Put 3 tablespoon of any milk powder to 1 cup of luke warm water. This method makes thick creamy yogurt.

GARAM MASALA MIXTURE
(whole)— Hot Spice

Always mix your own 'garam masala' mixture and keep it handy in a glass jar or bottle, as it is frequently required. Most housewives' recipes vary, but I prefer this one.

12 bay leaves
2 tablespoons black pepper corns
2 tablespoons black cumin seeds
2 tablespoons big black cardamoms
2 tablespoons cinnamon sticks (broken in pieces)

2 tablespoons cloves
2 tablespoons coriander seeds
2 tablespoons green cardamoms

GARAM MASALA POWDER
Powdered Hot Spice

This can be bought commercially but it is always better to make your own. Take a teaspoon full of each ingredient mentioned in the whole 'garam masala' mixture, except the bay leaves. Grind the spices in a coffee grinder together and store the powder in a glass bottle. Keep in the refrigerator for its fresh flavour.

GHEE
Clarified Butter

'Ghee' can be bought in many grocery shops but if one wants to be adventurous and enterprising, try making your own!

Heat 4 ozs of butter and let it simmer until all the water evaporates, it will take about half an hour. Remove from heat and strain the melted butter through a double layer of muslin cloth. Pour in a wide-necked glass jar and cool completely. Cover and store in a cool place or inside the fridge. You can make whatever quantity you want to make.

'Ghee' tastes best on hot chappatis and paranthas or as a 'baghaar' of ghee with cumin seeds and garlic poured over a dal (lentil).

IMLI PAANI
Tamarind water paste

Tamarind paste or dried tamarind is sold in Indian specialist shops all over the world. These days the paste is sold in small plastic jars. It is sold in a very concentrated form, so only about a teaspoon is required for a dish. But I prefer to make the dry tamarind pulp. Soak about 2 tablespoons of tamarind pulp in 1 cup of water for about an hour. Strain the water through a thick metal sieve. Discard the pulp and use the tamarind water.

Tamarind water is used mostly in south Indian recipes in dals, vegetables, rice, sambhar, dal curry and chutneys.

KHOA
Solidified milk

'Khoa' can be bought at a sweetmeat shop, and is sold by weight. It is always better to make your own fresh 'khoa'. Boil 6 cups of milk on a slow flame in a 'wok' for about 1-2 hours until all the liquid has been absorbed and a thick granular looking milk is left in the 'wok'. Cool and keep in the fridge.

It is mainly used in sweets or in rich party vegetable curries.

MALAI
Milk cream

'Malai' is the thick top layer of cream, which floats on top of full cream milk when heated. As the milk cools down a thick layer slowly starts forming. Collect the 'malai' by scooping it out with a spoon and keep it in a glass bowl with a cover. Repeat the process for about a day or two until about a cup of 'malai' is collected. It is good to whip it up with a little sugar for children. It can also be served with various sweets or mixed with a fruit salad or just grapes and 'malai'! It is full of calories, so beware, but nevertheless delicious!

MUNG DAL KE ANKUR
Mung bean sprouts

Mung bean sprouts are very healthy to eat in a vegetarian diet. They should be eaten at least thrice a week. They are highly nutritious. It takes about 48 hours to make your own sprouts. Soak about 1 cup of mung beans after cleaning them, in about 4 cups of water at night. Drain out the water in the morning and tie the soaked mung beans in a wet muslin cloth. Keep wetting the muslin throughout the day. Keep them tied until the next morning, the sprouts will be ready. Freeze them in a plastic bag or use them at once.

I love using them with yogurt as a salad.

NAARIYAL DUDH
Coconut milk

Coconut milk is used mostly in south India. It is cooked with vegetables, rice and sweets. Coconut milk can be made by grating a fresh coconut. Add 2 cups of boiling water over the grated coconut. Leave the mixture for about an hour. Sieve the mixture through a wet muslin cloth. Keep squeezing out as much liquid as possible until the pulp is completely dry. This liquid is called coconut milk. Discard the grated pulp.

PANCH FORAN
Five spice mixture

These days, one can buy the 'panch foran' mixture packet in specialist stores. If one has the spices at home, one can mix them and store them in a bottle. 'Panch' means five. This 'panch foran' is mostly used in 'baghaar' (seasoning) of certain vegetables. To make your own 'panch foran' mixture, mix together in a bowl the following:

1 tablespoon aniseed seeds
1 tablespoon cumin seeds
1 tablespoon fenugreek seeds
1 tablespoon mustard seeds
1 tablespoon nigella seeds

PANEER
Indian cheese

'Paneer' is an Indian cheese. It can be made very easily. These days it is sold in grocery shops also. To make your 'paneer' boil 4 cups of milk to boiling point. Add 4 tablespoons of lemon juice to the boiling milk. When the milk starts curdling, remove from fire and cool it. Pass the liquid through a muslin cloth and strain it. Squeeze out all the liquid and keep pressing. When all the liquid is drained out, press the 'paneer' inside the muslin cloth under a heavy utensil so that it gets completely drained dry. The 'paneer' gets ready after about an hour after pressing it. Put it in the fridge and cut into small cubes whenever you want to use it.

Paneer is like cottage cheese if it is crumbled instead of being cut into cubes. It is also very nutritious and a good source of proteins for vegetarians.

SAMBHAR POWDER

'Sambhar' is a south Indian dal curry. It is eaten in the south almost daily with boiled rice. The 'sambhar' powder can be bought but it is always better to make one's own. Each ingredient is roasted dry separately, and ground into powder separately. The ingredients are then mixed together and stored in an airtight bottle. Roast the following ingredients separately.

$1/4$ teaspoon asafoetida
1 teaspoon black green gram (urad dal)
1 teaspoon black pepper corns
1 teaspoon cinnamon sticks (broken pieces)
1 tablespoon coriander seeds
1 teaspoon cumin seeds
1 teaspoon desiccated coconut
$1/2$ teaspoon fenugreek seeds
5 red chillies (dried)
1 teaspoon split pea (chana) dal

Basic Indian Implements

A few important items are needed in an Indian kitchen. The items listed below are some of the implements required.

A set of 5 bhagonas with lids (Indian stainless steel pots)
2 large cooking spoons
1 flat spatula
1 slotted spoon for frying
1 pair of kitchen tongs
1 'tawa' (iron griddle for chappatis)
1 wooden rolling pin and board
1 'karahi' or 'wok' for deep frying (cast iron)
4 'thaalis' (big platters for eating)
2 jugs with lids
12 'katoris' (bowls for curry)
1 chappati box
1 spice box
1 small 'ghee' bowl with lid and spoon
1 'sarota' (for cutting betel nut and almonds etc.)
6 different sizes bowls
6 dishes to serve
2 rice platters
1 sieve
1 ordinary sieve for flour
1 potato peeler
5 knives of different sizes
1 chopping board for ginger, onions etc.
1 chopping board for fruits only
1 blender and mixer
1 coffee grinder
1 mortar and pestle
1 steaming pan
1 rice cooker
1 toaster oven
1 large pressure cooker
1 small pressure cooker
1 set 'idli' mould
1 non-stick 'dosa tawa'
1 steel or plastic grater
1 lemon squeezer
2 muslin cloths (1 metre each)
1 cheese cloth (1 metre)
2 tiffin carriers
1 bottle opener
2 alluminium or 'Hindolium' 'woks' (for cooking vegetables)

Weights & Measures

60 drops	1 teaspoon	2 teaspoons	1 dessert spoon
3 teaspoons	1 tablespoons	2 tablespoons	1 ounce (oz.)
16 tablespoons	1 cup	1 tea cup	4 to 5 oz.
2 cups	1 pint	4 cups	1 quart
1 pint	1 lb.	1 ounce	28.0 grams
16 ounces	1 lb.	1 lb.	453.6 gms.
1 kilogram	2.2 lbs.	1 kilogram	1000 gms.
50 gms.	1 3/4 ozs.	100 gms.	3 1/2 oz.
200 gms.	7 ozs.	250 gms.	8 3/4 oz.
500 gms.	17 1/2 oz.		

Equivalents

1 lb. sugar	2 cups	1 lb. flour	4 cups
1 lb. powder milk	2 1/2 cups	8 oz. liquid milk	1 cup
1 lb. fat	2 cups	1 oz baking powder	2 1/2 tablespoons
1 lb. chopped dry fruits	3 cups	1 lb. raw rice	1 cup
1 lb. sugar	2 1/2 cups	200 gms. dal	1 cup
200 gms sugar	1 cup	200 gms. rice	1 cup
150 gms. flour	1 cup		

Indian Measures

5 Tolas	= 1 chatak	4 chatak	= 1 pao
4 paos	= 1 seer	40 seer	= 1 mound

Aperitifs and Drinks

Apertifs & Drinks

Drinks are always served before a meal. Either dining at home or going out for a meal in a restaurant, drinks are always ordered before the main meal. Besides ordering any aerated drink or a whiskey, soda, gin and tonic, there is a variety of Indian drinks which can be ordered to start your evening on a threshold of the oncoming curry meal. In this chapter, you will have an ample choice of easy to make drinks to order or make at home.

Always make lemon juice cubes and keep in the fridge as they add to the flavour of some of the drinks. These drinks can also serve as an appetiser.

Mixed vegetable soup

Tomato soup

Pea pullao

Gatta pullao

Phulka, parantha, masala roti, aloo dal parantha & papad

Parantha & kaali dal

Cutlets & chips

Dosa, sambhar & coconut chutney

Apertifs & Drinks

Jal Jeera
CUMIN WATER

This drink is very popular before an Indian meal. It is also used as an accompaniment with the famous paani puris. It is very spicy and sour and can be kept in the fridge for about 3 days.

4 oz. dried tamarind
A few sprigs of fresh mint (ground)
½ teaspoon red chilli powder
½ teaspoon ground black salt
2 tablespoons lemon juice
1 tablespoon powdered jaggery or brown sugar

6 glasses cold water
2 teaspoons cumin powder
Salt to taste
½ teaspoon roasted cumin seed powder
6 lemon slices for garnishing

Soak tamarind in cold water for about 2 hours. Strain the liquid through a damp muslin cloth. Add the ingredients to the liquid and blend them all in the blender or mix it together with a whisk. Chill before serving. Put table salt on a plate, wet rims of the six glasses and dip them upside down in the plate of salt, so that the rims get coated with salt. Pour the Jal Jeera in the glasses and put the lemon wedge on the edge of the glass, sideways. Serve with ice cubes.

Serves: 6

Meethi Lassi Dilkhush
SWEET YOGURT SHAKE

This is a very refreshing drink on a cool midsummer night which can be made beforehand. Serve in tall glasses.

2 cups natural yogurt
2 tablespoons sugar
½ teaspoon cardamom powder

4 glasses cold water
½ teaspoon rose essence
A pinch of saffron (optional)

Put all the ingredients in a blender and blend them together. Serve this thick foamy drink in tall glasses.

Serves: 6

Apertifs & Drinks

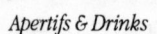

Namkeen Lassi
SALTY YOGURT SHAKE

This is served mostly in the mornings or at lunch time in the summer months. It is believed that 'namkeen lassi' prevents a sunstroke! It is a healthy drink and is easy to make. It is good for digestion too.

2 cups natural yogurt	4 glasses cold water
Salt to taste	A dash of black pepper powder
1 teaspoon roasted cumin seed powder	

Put all the ingredients in a blender and mix them well. Pour into a jug and serve.

Serves: 6

Gajjar Kaanji
CARROT WATER

This is a popular drink in North India. It is made in the winter months, when the black carrots are in season. It can also be made from ordinary carrots, but the deep purple colour of the 'kaanji' water will be missing. It is a tangy, salty drink. A few beetroot slices can be added to the ordinary carrot 'kaanji' to give it the right colour. This drink is usually made in an earthen pot. A good appetizer!

1 lb. black carrots	Salt to taste
2 tablespoons black mustard seeds (crushed)	
1 teaspoon red chilli powder	5 pints cold water

Peel the carrots and cut it into 6 long slices lengthwise. Wash them thoroughly. Add the spices to the carrots. Put all the carrots inside the earthen pot or glass jar. Pour cold water onto the carrots and spices. Tie a muslin cloth on top of the opening of the pot or jar. Place the pot in the sun for 2 or 3 days and keep shaking it daily. If there is no sunlight then keep the jar on the windowsill in the kitchen for a week. Stir it daily. Serve when ready in glasses with a slice of carrot in each glass. You can also store it in the fridge when ready.

Serves: A family of 4-6

Apertifs & Drinks

Tamatar ka Ras
TOMATO JUICE COCKTAIL

This is a great favourite when tomatoes are in season.

1 lb. tomatoes or 6 small tomato juice cans
6 glasses water
2 teaspoons Worcester sauce
Salt to taste
1/4 teaspoon red chilli powder
A dash of cream
2 teaspoons vinegar
2 teaspoons sugar
A dash of black pepper
1 tablespoon lemon juice

Cut the tomatoes and mix 6 glasses of water and blend or use the tomato juice. Mix all the ingredients in a cocktail shaker or blender, except the cream. Shake well. Serve chilled with a dollop of cream on top of each glass.

Serves: 6

Nimboo Shikanji
LEMON DRINK

'Nimboo Shikanji' or 'Nimboo Paani' is the most popular drink in India, and almost every home makes it in the summer months. It was popularised in the days of the Raj.

3 lemons
6 glasses water
A dash of black pepper (optional)
6 tablespoons sugar
Pinch of salt

Squeeze out the juice of the lemons. Dissolve the sugar in water and cook on a slow flame for about 10 minutes. Add salt and pepper and the sweet water to the lemon juice and stir. Serve chilled.

Serves: 6

Apertifs & Drinks

Neembu ka Sherbet
LEMONADE

This is a very refreshing drink and good to serve thirsty school children before meals.

6 lemons
6 tablespoons sugar
3 pints boiling water

Wipe each lemon with a damp cloth. Remove the rind from 3 lemons, as thinly as possible with a peeler. Cut the lemons into halves. Squeeze out the juice. Strain the juice into a jug. Add the lemon rind and sugar in the lemon juice. Then add the boiling water to the jug. Mix everything. Keep the jug covered and allow the lemonade to stand till cold. Strain it once again, and serve chilled.

Serves: 6

Imli ka Soda Paani
TAMARIND FIZZ

This drink is a sour drink and very refreshing in the summer. Serve it with lots of crushed ice.

4 ozs. tamarind
Salt to taste
1 teaspoon cinnamon powder
A few drops of red colour
1 tablespoon ginger-root (ground)
1 tablespoon sugar
4 cups boiling water
2 cups soda water

Put the tamarind, ginger-root, salt, sugar and cinnamon in a glass bowl. Pour in the boiling water. Cover and stand till cold. Strain through a damp muslin cloth into a jug. Add the red colour and stir. Chill in the fridge. Just before serving add the soda water and some crushed ice.

Serves: 6

Apertifs & Drinks

Aam ka Panna
MANGO WATER

This is a very popular in the summer months when the small green 'Kairees' (unripe green mangoes) are in season.

3 raw mangoes (peeled) 6 glasses of water
3 tablespoons of sugar Salt to taste
1 teaspoon roasted cumin seed powder
$1/2$ teaspoon chilli powder or black pepper powder

Boil the mangoes and separate the pulp. Mix the pulp with the water and sugar. Strain the liquid through a wet muslin cloth. Add the remaining ingredients and stir well. Chill before serving.

Serves: 6

Amras
SWEET MANGO DRINK

This drink is very popular in the summer. Make it in large jugs and keep in the fridge, whenever ripe mangoes are available. In some parts of India, it is eaten with 'puris'.

6 ripe mangoes 6 glasses of cold milk
6 tablespoons of sugar 6 green cardamoms (crushed)

Peel and cut the mangoes. Put the mango slices, cold milk, sugar and cardamoms into a blender and make into a smooth puree. Chill before serving in tall glasses.

Serves: 6

Apertifs & Drinks

Kharbooze ka Panna
MUSK MELON DRINK

A popular summer drink which acts as a coolant.

1 musk melon or cantaloupe	4 tablespoons sugar
1 teaspoon rose essence	6 glasses water
Some ice cubes	

Peel the musk melon and dice. Add sugar, rose essence and cold water and stir. Serve in tall glasses with ice cubes and a large spoon to eat the melon cubes with.

Serves: 6

Ananaas ka Sherbet
PINEAPPLE PUNCH

This is a refreshing fizzy drink and is lots of fun to serve at parties or at brunches.

$3/4$ cup lemon juice	$1 \, 1/2$ cups orange juice
$1/2$ cup sugar	6 pineapple slices (canned)
3 cans soda water	3 cans ginger ale

Mix the fresh lemon juice and orange juice with sugar in a bowl. Place the bowl in the fridge for about 2 hours. Keep it covered. Strain the punch and add the chopped pineapple slices, soda water and ginger ale. Mix with a large spoon. Serve in a punch bowl, with lots of crushed ice or ice cubes.

Serves: 12

Apertifs & Drinks

Masala Milk Shake
SPICY MILK SHAKE

This is a very nutritive drink. It can be served hot or cold, according to the season or personal choice.

6 glasses milk
1 teaspoon rose essence
A pinch of saffron
A few pistachios for garnish (sliced)

8 teaspoons sugar
1 teaspoon cardamom powder
12 almonds (skinned and ground)

Put the milk and all the ingredients together and blend. Pour in 6 clay pots (sikoras) or thick ceramic mugs or glasses. Garnish on top with the pistachios just before serving.

Serves: 6

Badaam ka Doodh
ALMOND MILK SHAKE

This is a very good drink for children during their examination days! It is said, in India, that almonds are very good for the brain and for good eyesight.

6 glasses of milk
6 green cardamoms (peeled and crushed)
12 teaspoons sugar

30 almonds (peeled and ground)

A pinch of saffron

Put the milk in a blender and add all ingredients. When thoroughly mixed, put into individual mugs and microwave them before serving. (About 5 minutes in the microwave). If you want to serve it cold, put the milk in a covered jug and put in the fridge. Stir before serving.

Serves: 6

Apertifs & Drinks

Ande ka Doodh
EGG FLIP

This hot milk drink is very nourishing in winters.

3 eggs
6 teaspoons sugar
1 teaspoon vanilla essence
6 cups hot milk
A dash of grated nutmeg

Beat the eggs in a bowl. Add milk and whisk with an electric beater. Add the remaining ingredients and beat them up together. The milk should be really hot. Serve in large mugs with some chocolate biscuits.

Serves: 6

Kele ka Doodh
BANANA MILK

6 ripe bananas
3 eggs
A dash of nutmeg
A pinch of salt
6 cups cold milk

Blend the banana along with all other ingredients in a blender until frothy. Serve it at once in crystal glasses.

Serves: 6

Apertifs & Drinks

Thandai
COOLING SPICED DRINK

It is made mostly in the month of May and June when the temperature outside is unbearable. It is made in most homes at teatime, instead of the usual hot, pot of tea! It's a very spicy drink.

8 almonds (soaked in water)
1 teaspoon poppy seeds
4 black pepper corns
$\frac{1}{2}$ teaspoon cinnamon powder
$\frac{1}{2}$ cup water to grind
3 cups cold milk
A few fresh pink rose petals, for garnish

8 pistachios (soaked in water)
1 teaspoon aniseeds
12 melon seeds
A pinch of nutmeg powder
2 cups cold water
6 teaspoons sugar

Peel the almonds and pistachios. Grind them to a thick paste along with all the other spices. Add cold water to the ground paste and mix well. Strain through a damp muslin cloth. Add the milk and sugar. Chill. Serve garnished with rose petals floating on top.

Serves: 6

Apertifs & Drinks

Thandi Chai
ICED TEA

This is a thirst quencher in the hot sunny days of the summer months.

6 cups water	3 teaspoons tea leaves
A few mint leaves	3 teaspoons lemon juice
3 teaspoons sugar	6 slices of lemon, for garnish
A few ice cubes	

Boil the water with tea and mint leaves. When ready, strain. Add lemon juice and sugar and chill. Just before serving, float a lemon slice on top of each cup or glass and add some ice cubes.

Serves: 6

Elaichi ki Chai
CARDAMOM TEA

This tea is delicious when it is served piping hot with a hot scone or bun. It is also good for a sore throat. "Chai Garam" (hot tea) are popular chanting words early in the morning at all railway stations in India.

3 teaspoons tea leaves	5 cups water
12 teaspoons sugar	1 cup milk
6 green cardamoms (crushed)	

Put all the ingredients in a pan and bring to a boil. Strain and serve hot in earthen ware pots or in ceramic mugs.

Serves: 6

Apertifs & Drinks

Thandi Coffee
COLD COFFEE

Good to serve at ladies' coffee mornings in small glasses.

6 teaspoons instant coffee	5 cups hot water
12 teaspoons sugar	2 cups cold milk
Dash of cream on top	or 6 spoons of vanilla ice-cream on top

Put the coffee powder in a jug. Pour hot water and sugar and mix well. Cool it completely. Add the milk and blend it in the blender. Serve it at once in tall glasses with a dollop of ice-cream on top. Cream or ice-cream can also be blended along with the coffee mixture if you wish.

Serves: 6

Naashte ke Pakwaan
– Snacks –

Naashte ke Pakwaan

'Naashta' means a snack. I will be giving a few recipes of some of them. Indian snacks are very palatable and popular. The snacks are mostly deep-fried. Snacks can be served as starters, at tea time or at cocktails or brunches. 'Samosas' and 'Bhajiyas' are very popular at all restaurants around the world.

Snacks are mostly served with an accompaniment of a chutney or sauce. Most chutneys are made from coriander, mango, mint, tamarind, onions, etc. These are specified with each snack. Tomato ketchup can be substituted for all chutneys. Snacks are also seasonal, as various vegetables are available only in the season.

Some people only eat snacks as a meal at dinner time, and it shows when the executive paunch starts appearing! So beware of our tasty fried friends—the Indian snacks.

Naashte ke Pakwaan

Saade Pakore
BASIC PLAIN PAKORAS

Plain Pakoras are very popular in India. These can be used in many other dishes like pakora curry, pakora raita, pakora karhi, etc.

1 cup besan (chickpea flour)	1 teaspoon baking power
1 teaspoon chilli powder	1 teaspoon 'garam masala' powder
Salt to taste	1 teaspoon 'anaardaana'
1 teaspoon coriander seeds	1 onion, chopped
1 cup oil, for frying	$1/_3$ cup water for mixing (approx.)

Mix the 'besan' flour with all the ingredients with water. Heat oil in a 'wok' and drop a spoonful of batter, about six at a time. Turn over the pakoras, when golden, drain on a paper towel. Serve hot with a coriander or mint chutney.

Serves: 6

Cheese Ke Bhajiye
CHEESE FRITTERS

This is a quick and easy snack to make for unexpected visitors.

3 ozs. cheddar cheese	3 ozs. self raising flour (sieved)
Salt to taste	1 teaspoon 'garam masala' powder
2 eggs (beaten)	3 ozs. milk
1 cup oil for frying	1 teaspoon baking powder

Grate the cheese and keep aside. In a bowl, put flour, salt, pepper, grated cheese, eggs and milk and make into a smooth paste. Add the baking powder and stir well. Leave the batter aside for about half an hour.

Heat the oil in a 'wok' and spoon out the batter about six at a time in the oil. Turn the fritters over until golden. Drain them with a slotted spoon on a paper towel.

Serve hot with ketchup.

Serves: 6

Naashte ke Pakwaan

Methi Pakora
FENUGREEK LEAVES PAKORAS

These pakoras taste well with a hot cup of tea.

1 cup 'besan' (chickpea flour)
1 small green chilli (chopped)
$\frac{1}{2}$ teaspoon red chilli powder
1 cup oil for frying
1 tablespoon peanuts, crushed
Salt to taste
1 small onion (chopped)
1 teaspoon 'garam masala' powder
A bunch of fenugreek leaves
$\frac{1}{3}$ cup water approx., for mixing

Make a batter with 'besan' flour and all the spices with water.

Wash and clean the fenugreek leaves and chop them coarsely. Mix the fenugreek leaves with the batter.

Heat oil in a 'wok'. Drop the batter with a spoon in the oil, about six at a time. Turn the pakoras over the other side until golden. Drain on a paper towel.

Serve with a coriander or mint chutney.

Serves: 6

Naashte ke Pakwaan

Aloo Matar Samosa
PEAS AND POTATO SAMOSA

Samosas are a triangular pastry filled with a filling. There are many varieties of fillings but the most popular one is with potatoes. Samosas can be made well in advance. They should be half fried and cooled. Put in a plastic bag and freeze. They can then be deep fried whenever required.

For the filling
1 tablespoon oil
1 onion, chopped
1 cup greenpeas (boiled or canned)
$1/2$ teaspoon red chilli powder
1 teaspoon mango powder
1 teaspoon cumin seeds
3 medium potatoes (boiled and cubed)
Salt to taste
1 green chilli (chopped)
1 teaspoon 'garam masala' powder

For the pastry shell
2 cups self raising flour
$1/2$ cup water for the dough (approx.)
2 tablespoons oil
1 cup oil for frying

Heat oil in a pan. Stir fry cumin seeds and chopped onion. Add the potatoes, peas and all the spices. Keep aside.

Make a dough by sifting the flour in a bowl. Add the oil and mix well. Then gradually add the water and make a stiff dough.

Divide the dough into 16 equal balls. Roll out each ball into a flat disc of about 4 inches in diametre. Before rolling them dip into some oil to avoid sticking.

Cut the disc into half. Fold the half disc into a triangular cone. Fill each cone with a teaspoon full of the potato filling. Stick the open end with water and seal it firmly. Make 32 samosas in the same way.

Heat oil in a 'wok', deep fry a few 'samosas' at a time. Drain them on a paper towel. Serve hot with coriander chutney.

Yields: 32

Naashte ke Pakwaan

Dal Ki Kachori
STUFFED PULSES SAVOURY PASTRY

'Kachoris' are very popular in India. They remain fresh for 2-3 days.

$1/4$ lb. split urad dal
Salt to taste
1 teaspoon pepper corns, crushed coarsely
1 teaspoon coriander seeds
4 tablespoons oil
1 teaspoon red chilli powder
2 cups oil for frying
1 lb. self raising flour
$3/4$ cup water (approx.)

    Wash and soak the dal overnight. Drain and grind it in the blender to a coarse paste. Mix the chilli powder, salt, pepper corns and coriander seeds.

    Mix the flour and oil together and rub well with your fingers. Slowly add water and make into a stiff dough. Knead thoroughly and keep aside for an hour. Knead again. Divide into equal sized balls, about 12 to 14. Make a slight depression in the centre and fill with a little dal paste. Cover the dal paste completely with the dough and flatten it between your palms. Roll lightly about 3 inches in diameter. Repeat the process until all are done.

    Heat oil in a 'wok' and fry a few at a time on a very low heat. Turn them over when golden brown, drain on a paper towel. These can be eaten hot or cold. Good for school lunches, picnics or journeys.

Yields: 12 to 14

Naashte ke Pakwaan

Dhokla
STEAMED RICE AND BEAN MUFFINS

'Dhoklas' is a Gujarati speciality. These are spongy savoury cake eaten at tea time or as a starter before a meal. They are served with a coriander and coconut chutney.

1 cup rice flour	1 cup cowpeas (black eyed beans)
2 cups hot water	2 tablespoons yogurt
Salt to taste	1 teaspoon red chilli powder
1 teaspoon turmeric powder	1 teaspoon 'Eno' fruit salt
2 tablespoons oil for garnish	1 green chilli chopped
1 teaspoon mustard seeds	12 curry leaves
1 tablespoon grated coconut	

Put the rice flour and the cowpeas in separate bowls and soak overnight in hot water. Drain the beans and remove the skins. Grind the flour, beans, yogurt and spices together. Add the 'Eno' fruit salt and mix well. Pour the mixture into a greased mould and steam for about 20 minutes, until the dhokla is cooked.

Heat oil and add the green chillies, mustard seeds, curry leaves and pour over the steamed dhokla. Unmould the dhokla and cut it into 2 inch square pieces. Sprinkle coconut on top. Serve each square with a teaspoonful of coriander and coconut chutney on top.

Serves: 6

Dahi Bhalla
YOGURT FRITTERS

Dahi Bhalla are very popular in most homes and restaurants.

For the Bhalla

2 cups split urad dal	$1/2$ cup chana dal
Salt to taste	1 green chilli, chopped
1 pinch of asafoetida	2 teaspoons oil
A few raisins	1 tablespoon cashewnuts, chopped

Naashte ke Pakwaan

2 cloves of garlic, chopped
For the yogurt sauce
2 cups natural yogurt
2 teaspoons sugar
1 teaspoon red chilli powder
For the chutney
1 cup water
1 tablespoon jaggery or brown sugar
½ teaspoon red chilli powder
1 teaspoon ginger-root, ground

2 cups oil, for frying

Salt to taste
1 teaspoon roasted cumin seed powder

2 tablespoons tamarind
1 tablespoon raisins
Salt to taste
A pinch of black salt (optional)
1 teaspoon cumin powder

Soak both the dals together for about 5 hours. Drain and then grind them into a fine paste. Add the salt, chilli, and all the other ingredients for the bhalla. Mix thoroughly. Grease your palms and make a round flat batter disc on your palm or on a small piece of banana leaf.

Heat oil for frying in a wok. Slowly slide the batter from your palm onto the oil. Be careful not to get burnt! Put about 3 'bhallas' in the hot oil. Turn them over and fry on both sides until golden.

Meanwhile keep a bowl of water (2 cups hot water and 1 teaspoon salt) ready. As you take them out of the oil, drop the bhallas into the hot salted water. Let them soak in the water for about 5 minutes. Then take out each bhalla and press it firmly between both your palms to squeeze out the water. Arrange them in a row on a deep serving dish.

Beat the yogurt with salt and sugar. Pour this yogurt over the bhalla evenly, covering them. Sprinkle the cumin and chilli powder on top of the yogurt in a nice pattern, either in alternate stripes or in a circular design. Use your own imagination!

To make the chutney, soak the tamarind and jaggery for about 1 hour. Sieve the tamarind paste. Add all the seasonings to the tamarind and mix well. Chill the chutney and the bhallas for about 2 hours before serving. Serve accompanied by a spoonful of chutney on top of each serving.

Serves: 6

Naashte ke Pakwaan

Aaloo Ki Tikki
POTATO PATTI

'Aaloo Ki Tikki' is a very popular snack. It is eaten with a sweet and sour tamarind chutney.

For the filling
2 green chillies	1 piece of ginger root
A bunch of coriander leaves	1 cup boiled peas
Salt to taste	

For the outer cover
1 lb. boiled potatoes	Salt to taste
1 tablespoon lemon juice	$\frac{1}{2}$ cup oil, for shallow frying

Grind the green chillies, ginger root and coriander leaves together. Mix this paste with the boiled peas and salt. Keep aside.

Mash the potatoes and mix salt and lemon juice. Make a small cup with the mashed potatoes and fill with a teaspoonful of the green peas mixture. Close slowly and firmly. Divide the potato mixture into 12 equal portions. Make all the potato tikkis in the same manner, and keep aside.

Heat a tava or a teflon pan. Grease it with a little oil. Place about four tikkis on the greased tava (iron griddle), shallow fry the tikkis until a crispy brown on one side, then turn it over and pour a teaspoon of oil and let the tikkis cook on the other side. Cook all the tikkis in the same manner.

Place two at a time in a serving plate and pour some tamarind chutney on top. Serve hot.

Serves: 6

Naashte ke Pakwaan

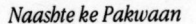

Bhel Puri
SPICY CRISPY RICE SNACK

Bhel Puri is a speciality of Bombay. I also fell victim to the addiction of bhel puri when I lived in Bombay. Try the recipe below for the taste of authentic bhel puri.

For the bhel
2 cups puffed rice or rice crispies
2 onions, chopped
1 cup fried 'besan' sev (thin fried needles)
1 green chilli, chopped
2 potatoes, boiled and cubed
1 cup papri, broken (fried white flour savoury biscuit)
1 cup fried chana dal (optional)
Salt to taste
Few green coriander leaves, chopped
1 teaspoon red chilli powder

For the chutney
1 cup tamarind water
2 teaspoons brown sugar
1 teaspoon ginger root, ground
Salt to taste
$1/2$ teaspoon red chilli powder
1 teaspoon garlic, ground

In a bowl mix all the ingredients of the bhel, and in another the chutney. Just before serving, dish it out in individual plates and pour some chutney on each plate. Add extra chillies as per individual taste.

Serves: 6

Naashte ke Pakwaan

Dahi Papri Chaat
YOGURT AND FRIED BISCUIT SAVOURY

This dish is my favourite snack! It can be prepared for a teatime snack and is a treat to serve to any guest.

For the Papri
2 cups self raising flour
Salt to taste
$1/2$ teaspoon carom seeds (optional)
2 tablespoons oil
$1/2$ cup water approx.
2 cups oil, for frying

For the yogurt sauce
2 cups yogurt
Salt to taste
1 teaspoon roasted cumin powder
1 tablespoon sugar
1 teaspoon red chilli powder
2 large potatoes, boiled & cubed

For the chutney
1 cup tamarind water (thick)
1 teaspoon red chilli powder
1 teaspoon garlic, ground
Salt to taste
1 tablespoon brown sugar
1 teaspoon ginger root, ground

Sift the flour in a bowl. Pour oil and salt and rub with your fingers. Slowly start pouring the water and knead it into a soft dough.

Roll out into a thin round disc. Cut out small inch discs with a biscuit cutter. Heat oil in a wok and fry the papris on a medium flame. Fry them on both sides until crisp. Drain them out on a paper towel. Repeat until all the papris are fried. Keep aside and allow to cool. These can be stored upto a fortnight in an airtight tin.

In another bowl, beat up the yogurt and add sugar, salt and other spices.

Take a quarter plate and arrange 5 papris in each plate, put a spoonful of boiled potato cubes over the papris, then pour some of the yogurt sauce over the papris and potatoes and cover them up. Repeat the same process in each plate.

Just before serving, pour a tablespoonful of tamarind chutney over the yogurt sauce. Try it out and see the smiles light up the faces of your guests!

Serves: 6 to 8

Naashte ke Pakwaan

Aaloo Chaat
SPICY POTATOES

This is a common, hot and spicy dish and can be made very easily.

6 potatoes, boiled, peeled and cubed
1 teaspoon roasted cumin seed powder
1 teaspoon roasted coriander seeds, crushed
1 teaspoon roasted dry red chillies, crushed
Salt to taste
$1/2$ teaspoon black salt
2 tablespoons lemon juice
1 teaspoon mango powder
1 green chilli, chopped
A few green coriander leaves, chopped

In a glass bowl, put the potatoes and all the ingredients. Mix well and chill before serving. Note: Chaat Masala bought commercially can also be substituted instead of roasting all the spices.

Serves: 6

Phalon Ki Chaat
SPICY FRUIT CHAAT

In this delicious dish the fruits have a curry, sweet and sour flavour! It is good to order in some Indian restaurants and easy to make at home.

2 apples, peeled and cubed
3 bananas, peeled and sliced
2 guavas, cubed
1 cup green grapes, seedless
3 tangerines or oranges, peeled and fleshed
2 teaspoons roasted cumin seed powder
1 teaspoon black pepper
$1/2$ teaspoon red chilli powder
Salt to taste
$1/2$ teaspoon black salt (optional)
1 teaspoon dried mint powder
1 teaspoon mango powder
1 teaspoon lemon juice
2 teaspoons sugar

Put all the fruits together in a glass bowl. Mix them all together with a salad fork and spoon. Mix all the ingredients in the fruits and toss it well. Chill a little before serving

Serves: 6

Naashte ke Pakwaan

Masala Dosai
STUFFED RICE PANCAKES

'Dosai' is a rice pancake which has been popularised all over the world. It is a south Indian dish. 'Dosai' can be eaten plain with a coconut chutney and sambhar (lentil curry) or stuffed with a potato filling hence calling it Masala Dosai'. It is made of a fermented batter of rice and lentils.

3 cups rice, uncooked + 3 cups water
1 cup urad dal (black gram) + 1 cup water
$1/2$ cup water approx. for mixing
Salt to taste

For the Filling
2 tablespoons oil
1 teaspoon chana dal or urad dal
1 large onion, sliced
1 teaspoon red chilli powder
Salt to taste
1 teaspoon mustard seeds
A few curry leaves
1 teaspoon turmeric powder
1 tablespoon lemon juice
4 large potatoes, boiled and cubed

For frying
1 cup 'ghee' or oil

Soak the rice and urad dal in water separately for about 6 hours. Drain water. Grind separately. Mix rice and dal together in a bowl, add salt, cover with a damp cloth and let it ferment overnight on the kitchen counter. The next morning, mix the water to obtain a thick consistency. Keep aside.

Heat oil in a pan and add the mustard seeds, chana dal and curry leaves and stir fry for half a minute. Then add the onions and sauté them for about 2 minutes. Add all the spices and cook for another 2 minutes. Lastly add the potatoes and mix. Keep this filling aside.

Heat a teflon 'Dosai Tawa' or an iron griddle and grease it with a little ghee or oil. Pour 2 tablespoons of the rice and lentil batter on the tawa and quickly spread it evenly into a circle of about 6 inches. Flatten it with the bottom of the spoon. Pour a tablespoon of oil around the edges of the dosai so that it does not stick to the bottom. It is a tricky affair. But with practice and a few unsuccessful attempts, one can master the technique of making dosais! Cover the dosai for a minute with a lid and then flip it over to cook on the other side. Remove onto an individual plate, spoon out some of the potato filling on to the centre of the dosai and fold into half. Serve it hot. Repeat the process until all are cooked. Serve with a coconut chutney and a bowl of piping hot sambhar as an accompaniment.

Serves: 6

Naashte ke Pakwaan

Idli
STEAMED RICE AND LENTIL CAKES

Idlis are a very popular south Indian breakfast dish. It is faster to make than a dosai. Idli can be eaten with a coconut chutney or sambhar (lentil curry) or with just melted hot ghee and sugar! They are light spongy rice and dal cakes, and are pure white in colour.

1 cup split urad dal
Salt to taste
$\frac{1}{2}$ cup water for mixing (approx.)

3 cups rice, uncooked
1 teaspoon baking powder

Clean the dal and soak it in 2 cups of water, for 8 hours. Soak the rice for 1 hour. Drain the urad dal and grind it to a fine paste. Drain the rice and grind it coarsely. Do not add any extra water to the paste. Mix both the pastes together and cover. Place the bowl in a warm place overnight, to ferment. Add the salt and baking powder the next morning. Mix it well and add half a cup of water, so that it becomes of a thick pouring consistency. Beat the idli batter with an electric hand beater. Grease the traditional idli moulds or an egg poacher. Pour the batter into the moulds. Stack the idli mould in three tier layers. Place the idli mould rack in a steaming pot with water. See that the water does not touch the idlis. Cover with a tight lid and steam for about 10 minutes. When ready, gently unmould the idli onto a thaali (platter). Repeat the process until all the batter is made into idlis. Serve at once with a coconut chutney, sambhar, hot lemon pickle or melted ghee and sugar.

Note: You can buy an 'idli' mould in any Indian grocery store.

Serves: 6

Naashte ke Pakwaan

Madrasi Vadai
LENTIL FRITTERS

1 ½ cups split urad dal
2 green chillies, chopped
6 curry leaves, chopped
Salt to taste

1 tablespoon chana dal (soaked for 1 hr.)
1 teaspoon ginger root, chopped
A few green coriander leaves, chopped
2 cups oil, for frying

Soak the urad dal for about 2 hours in a cup of water. Drain excess liquid. Grind to a paste and place in a bowl. Add the drained chana dal and all other spices and mix well with a fork or your hand. The batter should be stiff. Place a spoonful of batter on a greased banana leaf or greased paper and flatten it with the hand. Make a hole in the centre of the batter. Heat oil in a wok and slide the vadai batter into the hot oil. Fry on both sides until golden. Drain and serve hot with a coconut chutney.

Serves: 6

Mung Phalli ka Upma
GROUNDNUT UPMA

This south Indian snack is usually eaten at brunch or tiffin time. It is highly nutritious.

2 cups groundnuts or peanuts
1 tablespoon ghee
2 green chillies, chopped
1 teaspoon asafoetida
½ cup grated coconut
2 teaspoons lemon juice

3 cups water
1 teaspoon mustard seeds
1 onion, sliced
A pinch of turmeric powder
Salt to taste
A few coriander leaves, for garnish

Boil the peanuts in water for about 20 minutes. Drain and coarsely blend the peanuts in a blender. Heat ghee and fry the mustard seeds, chillies, onion, turmeric and asafoetida. Add the peanuts and coconut. Mix well. Cover the mixture and cook for about 5 minutes. Uncover and stir fry. Add the coriander and lemon juice and mix. Serve with a lemon pickle.

Serves: 6

Naashte ke Pakwaan

Chaklis
FRIED SAVOURY RINGS

This dish is very popular in southern India.

2 cups rice flour	1 cup besan (chickpea flour)
Salt to taste	1 tablespoon red chilli powder
$1/2$ teaspoon asafoetida	2 tablespoons sesame seeds, washed
2 tablespoons ghee or butter	$3/4$ cup water approx.
2 cups oil, for frying	

In a large bowl, mix all the ingredients. Rub well. Gradually, add the water and make into a soft dough. Heat oil in a wok. Make small portions of the dough. Place the ball of dough into a chakli press or a Sawa cookie press and hold it over the hot oil. Press the lever so that the dough is pushed out through the hole and makes a circle of the piped dough in the hot oil like a coil pattern, about 3 inches in size. Break the remaining dough in the container with your finger and lift off the press. Form another dough circle in the same manner. Quickly turn the chaklis over when golden and drain them on a paper towel. Repeat until all are fried.

Cool completely and store in an airtight tin or jar. These can be stored for about 2 to 3 weeks. They are good for nibbles at a cocktail party or on journeys and picnics.

Yields: 16-20

Naashte ke Pakwaan

Matthi
SALTY CRACKERS

'Matthis' are a snack which can be stored in an airtight container. Matthis are usually eaten with a mango pickle. This twin combination is also good on a train journey.

2 cups self raising flour
$\frac{1}{2}$ cup 'ghee'
1 tablespoon black pepper corns, ground coarsely
1 cup oil for frying
Salt to taste
$\frac{1}{3}$ cup water approx.

Sift the flour and salt in a bowl. Rub the ghee in the flour with your finger tips. Add the black pepper and mix well. Slowly add the water and make a stiff dough.

Divide the dough into 16-18 equal parts. Roll out each ball of dough into a thick disc, about 3 inches in diametre. Prick on one side with a fork. After rolling out all the discs, deep fry them on slow heat, in oil. Turn them over. When golden brown, drain them. Fry only 4 at a time. Cool them completely. Store them in an airtight tin or box.

Yields: 16 to 18

Aaloo aur Roti ka Upma
POTATO AND BREAD UPMA

2 tablespoons oil
A few curry leaves
1 cup boiled potatoes, cubed
Salt to taste
1 tablespoon lemon juice
1 teaspoon mustard seeds
1 green chilli, chopped
1 cup bread, cut into cubes
1 teaspoon red chilli powder
$\frac{1}{4}$ cup water

Heat oil in a wok. Add the mustard seeds and curry leaves. Then add the green chilli and stir fry for a minute. Add the potatoes, bread and all the spices except the lemon juice. Mix the lemon juice in water and keep on sprinkling it at regular intervals. Keep on stir frying until all the liquid is absorbed. Serve hot, with a lemon pickle.

Serves: 6

Naashte ke Pakwaan

Chaawal aur Aaloo Roll
RICE AND POTATO ROLL

This is a good snack at teatime when one is ravenously hungry after a day's work. It is very filling. It is also recommended for cocktail parties, served speared with a toothpick with a ketchup dip.

2 cups rice, cooked
1 egg, hard boiled
For the filling
2 tablespoons oil
2 onions, chopped
1 green chilli, chopped or
Salt to taste
For the batter
1 cup flour
Salt to taste
1 cup oil for frying

1 cup potatoes, boiled and mashed
$1/2$ cup water

1 teaspoon cumin seeds
1 bunch green coriander, chopped
1 teaspoon red chilli powder
1 tablespoon lemon juice

$1/2$ cup water
1 cup bread crumbs

Grind the rice, potatoes and the egg into a thick paste in the blender with water. Keep aside.

Put oil in a pan. Add cumin seeds, allowing them to brown. Add the onions and sauté for about 2 minutes. Add the rest of the ingredients of the filling and stir fry for about 5 more minutes. Keep aside.

Divide the mixture into 16-20 equal portions. Make a hollow in each portion and fill it with the onion filling. Close up the opening and shape them into round balls.

Next make a batter by mixing the flour, water and salt. Keep the bread crumbs on a plate.

Dip each potato ball into the batter and then roll it around in bread crumbs. Repeat the process until all the potato balls are coated in the bread crumbs. Keep them on a plate.

Heat oil in a wok and drop in about five pieces at a time. Keep turning them until they are golden brown evenly. Drain them on a paper towel. Serve them piping hot, with ketchup or a sweet chilli sauce.

Yields: 16-20

Naashte ke Pakwaan

Khandwi Rolls
SAVOURY YOGURT AND GRAM FLOUR ROLLS

2 cups yogurt
4 green chillies, ground
1 tablespoon ginger root, ground
Salt to taste

2 cups water
2 cups besan (chickpea or gram flour)
1 teaspoon turmeric powder

For garnishing
1 tablespoon oil
2 tablespoons coconut, grated
2 tablespoons green coriander leaves, chopped

1 teaspoon mustard seeds

Beat the yogurt in a bowl with a whisk and add water. Mix well. Gradually add the besan and stir till all the lumps disappear. Add chilli, ginger paste, turmeric and salt. Stir well. Pour the mixture into a large saucepan and cook on a slow flame, stirring all the time. Cook until it thickens to a thick custard consistency. Remove from fire and pour the mixture onto a greased cookie sheet. Let it cool completely. Then cut into strips and roll each strip. Carefully place each roll onto a serving platter and keep aside.

Heat oil in another pan and add the mustard seeds until they pop. Pour the oil and mustard seeds over the 'Khandwi' rolls. Sprinkle the coconut and coriander leaves on top of the rolls, just before serving. They taste delightful!

Serves: 6

Naashte ke Pakwaan

Bhutte aur Aaloo Ke Cutlets
CORN AND POTATO CUTLETS

These are a nice snack to serve for brunch or at tea time. They taste good with a coriander chutney or ketchup.

6 corn on the cobs
1 teaspoon cumin seeds
2 cloves of garlic, chopped
1 green chilli, chopped
4 large potatoes, boiled and mashed
1 teaspoon red chilli powder
1 tablespoon lemon juice

For the batter
1 cup flour
1 cup bread crumbs

2 tablespoons oil
1 onion, chopped
1 teaspoon ginger root, chopped
2 tablespoons besan or white flour
Salt to taste
A few green coriander leaves, chopped
1 cup milk

$1/2$ cup milk approx.
1 cup oil, for frying

Peel the corn and wash. Grate and keep aside. Heat oil in a deep pan and add cumin seeds until they brown. At once add onion, garlic, ginger root, and green chilli and sauté for 5 minutes. Quickly stir in the besan or white flour and stir. Add the milk and grated corn to the pan and cover. Let the corn cook for about 10 to 15 minutes on a medium flame, until the liquid dries up. Add the mashed potatoes and mix.

Mix salt, chilli powder, coriander leaves and lemon juice, into the mixture. Divide the mixture into 12 portions. Make into oval cutlet shapes and keep aside.

Make a batter with flour and milk. Dip each cutlet into the batter and then roll in bread crumbs. Keep them all on a large platter.

Heat oil in wok and deep fry two cutlets at a time. Stir carefully so as not to break them. Drain on a paper towel and serve hot.

Serves: 6

Naashte ke Pakwaan

Baigan ke Cutlets
EGGPLANT OR AUBERGINE CUTLETS

3 medium eggplants (aurbergines)   1 teaspoon vinegar
2 cups water   Salt to taste
For the filling
2 tablespoon oil   1 onion, chopped
1 tablespoon self raising flour   Salt to taste
$1/2$ teaspoon black pepper   1 tablespoon Worcester sauce
$1/2$ cup bread crumbs sautéed in 1 teaspoon of butter

Cut the eggplants into half. Put vinegar in water along with salt and boil the eggplants for about 10 minutes, until tender. Drain them out. Scoop out the inside pulp of the eggplant pulp and keep aside.

Heat oil in a pan, add the onions and sauté them until brown. Add the flour and stir it quickly. Then add all the seasoning, along with the mashed eggplant pulp.

Stuff this cooked mixture into the eggplant shells and press firmly with a spoon. Sprinkle the sautéed bread crumbs on top of all the 6 eggplant cutlets and press evenly with a knife. Make a checked square pattern on the crumbs with a knife. Bake the eggplant cutlets in the oven for about 10 minutes. Serve hot with butter sandwiches.

Serves: 6

Naashte ke Pakwaan

Bhutte ka Toast
CORN ON TOAST

1 tablespoon oil
1 teaspoon self raising flour
Salt to taste
1 teaspoon sugar
1 teaspoon lemon juice
1 cup oil for frying
1 onion, chopped
1 can of corn, drained
A dash of pepper
1 teaspoon butter
1 tablespoon cream (optional)
6 slices of bread
A few coriander or parsley leaves, chopped, for garnish

Heat oil in a pan, sauté the onions and add the flour. Stir in the drained corn along with all the seasonings and remove from heat, mix the cream and keep aside. Heat oil in a wok. Cut the bread slices into two pieces each. Fry each piece in hot oil and drain them on a paper towel. Arrange on a large serving platter and put the corn mixture on top of each piece. Garnish with chopped coriander leaves or parsley. Serve hot.

Serves: 6

Aaloo ke Kebab
POTATO KEBABS

This dish is easy to prepare and very tasty. It can be served at cocktails or tea parties. Serve these kebabs speared on toothpicks with a hot chutney.

1 lb. potatoes, boiled, peeled & mashed
1 egg, beaten
1 teaspoon red chilli powder
1 teaspoon roasted cumin seeds
1 green chilli, chopped
1 tablespoon lemon juice
3 tablespoons grated cheese
Salt to taste
2 tablespoons besan (chickpea flour)
1 teaspoon baking powder
A few coriander leaves, chopped
1 cup oil, for frying

In a large bowl, combine the potatoes and all the other ingredients and mix well. Heat oil in a wok. Drop spoonful of the potato mixture into the hot oil and fry on both sides. Fry about 5 at a time. Drain on a kitchen towel. Serve piping hot with a chutney.

Serves: 6

Naashte ke Pakwaan

Dahi Toast
YOGURT TOAST

This dish is a good starter for special occasions, or when you are entertaining a small group.

6 slices bread	3 eggs
1 teaspoon red chilli powder	1 teaspoon coriander powder
½ teaspoon turmeric powder	Salt to taste
1 cup yogurt	A few coriander leaves, chopped
1 teaspoon roasted cumin seeds	A pinch of salt
1 cup oil for frying	

Cut the bread into 6 round shapes. Beat the eggs in a bowl and mix all the spices and salt. Soak all the bread in the egg batter. Heat oil and fry the bread pieces on both sides. Drain on a paper towel. Beat up the yogurt in a separate bowl and mix the coriander leaves, cumin and salt. Pour the yogurt mixture over the fried bread, after arranging them on a large platter.

Serves : 6

Cheese Straws

These can be made in advance and served at cocktail parties, etc. Cheese straws can be stored in an airtight box.

3 oz. self raising flour	½ teaspoon salt
1 teaspoon red chilli powder	1 ½ oz. butter
2 oz. grated cheese	1 egg
½ cup water to mix (approx.)	

Sift the flour and salt in a bowl. Add the red chilli powder. Rub in the butter and cheese into the flour. Add the egg and gradually mix the water to form a stiff dough.

Roll into 4 inch long pieces. Trim edges using a sharp knife dipped in flour. Cut off narrow straws. Twist them in the centre like bow. Bake in an oven at 400° for about 7 to 10 minutes.

Cheese straws can also be deep fried instead of baked.

Naashte ke Pakwaan

Namkeen Kaaju
SALTY CASHEWNUTS

These nuts are a favourite feature of most elite bars in luxury hotels all over India. Sparkling silver bowl of hot salty cashewnuts is brought in when you order a Bloody Mary, Gin tonic or perhaps a fizzy soda. They taste better when served warm. Good as a snack with any apperitif.

1 cup oil for frying
1 teaspoon salt
$1/2$ teaspoon red chilli powder
$1/2$ lb. raw cashewnuts
$1/2$ teaspoon black pepper

Heat oil in wok. Add cashewnuts and fry for 5 minutes. Keep stirring all the time until they turn into a golden colour. Using a slotted spoon, drain the fried cashewnuts on a paper towel. Mix salt, black pepper and red chilli powder. Transfer onto a large plate and cool completely. Store in an airtight jar.

Pyaaz Ke Bhajiye
ONION BHAJIYAS

Onion 'Bhajiyas' are very popular. These are commercially sold all over England in pre-packed packages, especially Harrods.

2 large onions
Salt to taste
1 teaspoon garam masala powder
$1/2$ cup water to mix (approx.)
1 tablespoon fresh coriander leaves (chopped)
1 cup besan (chickpea flour)
1 teaspoon red chilli powder
1 teaspoon baking powder
1 cup oil for frying

Cut the onions in thick $1/2$ inch rings and keep aside. Sift the flour, add all the ingredients and mix the batter with water into a thick paste. Add more water if necessary. Heat oil in a 'wok'. Dip each onion ring in the 'besan' batter and deep fry on both sides. When golden brown, take it out with a slotted spoon and drain on a paper towel. Fry one onion ring a time until all are fried. Serve hot with ketchup or a coriander chutney.

Serves: 6

Shorbe

Shorbe
—Soups—

Shorbe

'Shorba' means soup. Soups are popular with the elite class or when ordering in a restaurant. South Indians like to eat their thin soups with their rice. It is a very economical dish. Soups are not part of the daily diet and are made only occasionally, when one is sick in bed or while eating out.

Shorbe

Matar ka Shorba
PEA SOUP

This soup is usually made in the winter months when peas are in season, and are easily available.

1 cup peas, shelled
Salt to taste
1 tablespoon lemon juice

6 cups of water
$1/2$ teaspoon black pepper corns, crushed
2 tablespoon cream, for garnish

Boil the peas in water with salt and pepper. Let it boil until the peas are soft. Put the soup in the blender. Add lemon juice. Re-heat the soup and pour into individual 6 portions. Top each serving with a dash of cream.

Serves: 6

Aaloo ka Shorba
POTATO SOUP

This soup is a favourite of most children as potatoes are a universal favourite.

4 potatoes, peeled and cubed
4 cups water
$1/2$ teaspoon red chilli powder
3 teaspoons minced parsley, for garnish

2 onions, sliced
Salt to taste
1 tablespoon butter
1 cup hot milk

Put the potatoes and onions in water and bring to a boil. Add the seasoning. Boil for about half an hour until the onions and potatoes are cooked. Sieve the soup. Stir in the butter and re-heat, bring to a boil and add the hot milk to the soup. Pour into individual bowls and garnish with parsley on top. Serve it very hot. You can serve it with some cream cracker biscuits or buttered bread.

Serves: 6

Shorbe

Chaawal ka Shorba
RICE SOUP

This soup is good to serve to convalescing people as it is easy to digest and is very easy to prepare.

3 onions, chopped
1 cup raw rice
Salt to taste
3 cups of water
2 cups tomatoes, peeled and chopped
A dash of pepper

Put the onions in a pan of water and boil for about 10 minutes. Then add the washed rice, tomatoes and the seasoning. Boil until the rice is cooked, for about half an hour. Serve hot.

Serves: 6

Tamatar aur Kothmir Rasam
TOMATO AND CORIANDER SOUP

This is a soup from the South. It is delicious and can be served before a meal as a soup or served along with rice during the meal. In the south, people eat rice with many different things. Rice is eaten with sambhar, with rasam and also with yogurt.

2 tablespoons oil
6 curry leaves
6 tomatoes, chopped
1 teaspoon black pepper corns, crushed
1/2 cup green coriander leaves, chopped, for garnish
1 teaspoon cumin seeds, crushed
1 teaspoon garlic, crushed
Salt to taste
4 cups of water

Heat oil in a pan, add the crushed cumin seeds and mustard seeds. Then quickly add the curry leaves, garlic and tomatoes and stir fry for a minute. Then add the seasoning and water. Simmer for about 15 minutes until the tomatoes are cooked. Either serve the rasam as it is or strain it. Add the coriander leaves last and stir them in just before serving. Serve the rasam hot.

Serve: 6

Shorbe

Pyaaz ka Shorba
ONION SOUP

This is a good soup to serve at parties. It is easy to make and is very different.

- 2 tablespoons oil or butter
- 3 large onions, chopped
- 1 teaspoon pepper
- 1 cup of milk
- 2 tablespoons cheese, grated
- 1 tablespoon corn flour or self raising flour
- Salt to taste
- 4 cups of water
- 1 onion, sliced and fried, for garnish

Heat butter or oil in a pan. Brown some cornflour or flour in the oil. Add at once the onions and sauté them for about 5 to 10 minutes. Add the seasoning and water. Simmer the soup for about 20 to 30 minutes. Strain the soup. Reheat it with milk. Pour in individual bowls and garnish each bowl with some fried onions and grated cheese. Serve hot.

Serves: 6

Shorbe

Gobhi ka Shorba
CAULIFLOWER SOUP

This is made in the winter months in India when cauliflower is in season. Many preparations are made from this versatile vegetable.

2 tablespoons butter or oil
1 cup milk
½ teaspoon red chilli powder
2 cups hot water
1 medium size cauliflower, cut into small flowerets.

2 tablespoons self raising flour
Salt to taste
A dash of pepper

Heat butter in a pan and stir in the flour. Add the milk and stir briskly. Add the seasoning and simmer for 5 minutes. Add the hot water and cauliflower and cook the soup for about 20 minutes, until the cauliflower is cooked. Serve in individual bowls. Serve it hot.

Serves: 6

Ande ke Pakwaan
— Egg Cookery —

Ande ke Pakwaan

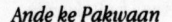

Eggs are eaten by most vegetarians. Eggs are used in so many different ways. In some houses eggs are prepared at dinner-time.

Egg is a very versatile item in cooking. Some people who are vegetarians but eat eggs, claim to be called as Eggetarians!

Ande ke Pakwaan

Bharwa Ande
STUFFED EGGS

This is an easy dish to prepare and is very appealing to the eyes as well as the palate..

6 eggs, hard boiled	1 tablespoon cheese, grated
Salt to taste	1 teaspoon pepper or red chilli powder
$1/2$ teaspoon mustard powder	1 teaspoon sugar
1 teaspoon lemon juice	2 tablespoons cold milk or cream
To decorate	
1 tomato	2 leaves of lettuce, cut into thin strips
Few leaves of mint	

Peel the eggs. Cut them into halves, lengthwise. Scoop out the yolk and put in a bowl. Mash the yolks again and add cheese and all the other ingredients. Mix well with a fork. Stuff the yolk mixture back into the boiled whites, with a knife, and press firmly. Dip the knife in cold water and smoothen the top of the stuffed eggs. Place them in an oval serving platter.

Wash the tomato and cut 12 small half inch diamond shapes. Place one tomato diamond in the centre of each egg. Wash the mint leaves and place 1 mint leaf beside each tomato on top of the stuffed egg. Decorate the sides of the platter with strips of lettuce. Keep in the fridge to chill for about an hour before serving.

Serves: 6

Ande ke Pakwaan

Ande aur Gobhi ke Pakore
EGG AND CAULIFLOWER FRITTERS

The fritters serve as an accompaniment to the main meal.

4 eggs
1 onion, chopped finely
1 teaspoon baking powder
1 cauliflower, cut into florets

$1/2$ cup white flour or corn flour
Salt to taste
1 teaspoon chilli powder
2 cups oil, for frying

Break the eggs in a bowl and beat with an egg beater. Mix the ingredients mentioned above except the cauliflower flowerets. Make a thick batter.

Heat oil in a wok. Dip each cauliflower floweret into the egg batter and deep fry in hot oil. Drain on a paper towel. Serve hot or cold with a mint chutney.

Serves: 6

Katori ke Ande
BAKED EGGS IN BOWLS

This dish can be served with bread and butter sandwiches for brunch, a late night T.V. supper, or as a first course.

6 'Katoris'
6 eggs
1 teaspoon red chilli powder
6 teaspoons butter

6 teaspoons oil, to grease the bowls
Salt to taste
6 tablespoons milk
6 teaspoons grated cheese

Take 6 bowls and grease them with a teaspoon of oil each. Break one egg in each bowl. Sprinkle salt and all the other ingredients equally into each bowl. Do not mix. Put the bowls on an oven tray and bake them at 300°C. for about 10-15 minutes. Check the eggs to see if they are cooked. Remove them from the oven and serve them placed in individual plates.

Serves: 6

Ande ke Pakwaan

Sunheri Ande
GOLDEN EGGS

This is an economical dish for brunches or suppers.

For golden egg
4 eggs, hard boiled, peeled
1 cup oil for frying

4 slices white bread, cut into 4 triangles
2 cups white sauce

For Sauce
2 tablespoons oil
2 tablespoons white flour
2 cups milk
1 tablespoon lemon juice

A dash of pepper
Salt to taste
1 teaspoon mustard powder

To make the white sauce: Heat oil in a pan. Stir in white flour. Take the pan off the fire and pour milk. Stir briskly, so that lumps do not form. Add pepper, salt and mustard paste or powder. When the sauce thickens, take off from the flame strain the white sauce through a sieve. Pour lemon juice and stir.

For the golden egg: Cut the hard boiled eggs into small pieces. Separate the boiled yolks and keep aside in a small bowl.

Mix the boiled egg whites in the white sauce. Meanwhile heat oil in a wok and deep fry the bread triangles croutons. Drain the croutons on a paper towel.

When all are fried, add them to the white sauce also and mix.

Pour this on to a flat oven serving plate. Crumble the boiled yolks with your fingers, in the bowl. Sprinkle the crumbled yolks over the white sauce. Cover the whole surface. It will then become golden egg! Serve hot with a bowl of tomato ketchup.

Serves: 6

Ande ke Pakwaan

Angrezi Anda Galantine
ENGLISH EGG GALANTINE

This is a light supper dish.

2 cups white sauce (see Golden Egg)
6 eggs, hard boiled
1 tablespoon butter
1 teaspoon red chilli powder or paprika
1/2 cup tomato sauce
2 tablespoons cheese, grated
1 tablespoon cream

Put the white sauce in a pyrex baking dish and add tomato sauce. Peel the boiled eggs, cut into quarters and mix into the sauce. Sprinkle the cheese on top. Put pats of butter and cream over the cheese and sprinkle the paprika on top. Put the dish under the broiler for about 5 minutes. Serve hot, with bread, butter and a salad.

Serves: 6

Ande ki Akuri
CURRIED SCRAMBLED EGGS

This is an instant dish to prepare wherever a quick meal is required. 'Akuri' on toast or 'Akuri' eaten with 'paranthe' (fried chappati) is very popular for breakfast or supper. It is tastier than the plain traditional scrambled eggs.

6 eggs
1 teaspoon cumin seeds
1 tomato, chopped
1 green chilli, chopped
1/4 cup coriander leaves, chopped
1 tablespoon butter
1 onion, chopped
1 teaspoon red chilli powder
Salt to taste
1/2 cup milk

Break the eggs in a bowl and whisk them. Heat the butter in a pan and add cumin seeds. When they are brown add onions and sauté for a minute. Pour the beaten egg with all the other ingredients. Keep stirring until the eggs curdle and form soft scrambled eggs. Serve on a flat platter with buttered toast or parantha.

Serves: 6

Ande ke Pakwaan

Desi Omelette
INDIAN OMELETTE

This egg dish is eaten all over India. The mild or hotter flavour depends upon the cook from different regions! This omelette can be cut into pieces and put into a curry gravy or put inside a sandwich or rolled inside a chappati with butter, or the omelette mixture can be poured over bread and fried in a griddle on both sides. This is a versatile recipe.

6 eggs
1 teaspoon cumin seeds
Salt to taste
$1/2$ cup coriander leaves, chopped
1 tomato, chopped
2 tablespoons cheese, grated (optional); or
2 tablespoons paneer, crumbled (optional)

1 onion, chopped
1 teaspoon chilli powder
2 spring onions, chopped (optional)
1 green chilli, chopped
$1/2$ cup oil, for frying

Break the eggs in a large bowl and beat with an egg whisk. Add all the ingredients and mix well.

Heat a non-stick frying pan and put a tablespoon of oil. Pour $1/3$ of the egg mixture into the frying pan. Spread evenly.

Fold three times and turn the omelette over. Press the omelette firmly on both sides with a spatula. Take it out and cut into 2 pieces. Repeat until all the omelettes are made.

Serve them hot. Even cold omelettes taste good in a sandwich or as an omelette burger!

Serves: 6

Ande ki Biryani
EGG AND RICE BIRYANI

This is a special dish from Hyderabad. It is delicious and is a meal in itself. Serve it with a dahi ki chutney (yogurt salad).

6 hard boiled eggs
1/2 lb french beans, boiled in salted water
2 cups Basmati rice
1 cup yogurt with 1 teaspoon salt mixed in 1 tablespoon garam masala powder
1/4 cup lemon juice
2 tablespoons raisins
1/4 cup hot milk mixed with 1 1/2 teaspoon saffron
2 tablespoon almonds, soaked, peeled, sliced
1/2 cup coriander leaves, chopped
4 cups water
1/2 cup ghee, melted
1/2 cup sliced fried onions

Peel the eggs and cut them into halves. Keep aside. Drain the beans and keep aside. Wash and clean the rice. Soak it for about an hour before cooking in water.

Take a large corning ware dish and grease it with a tablespoon of ghee. Put a layer of the cooked rice, a layer of the 3 halves eggs and a layer of half the beans.

Mix the yogurt with salt and garam masala powder. Pour half the yogurt mixture over the beans in the pan. Then pour half the lemon juice, sprinkle half the amount of fried onions, half raisins, half the amount of saffron milk, almonds and coriander leaves. Repeat the process by putting the rice layer first and so on. When everything is put in the second layer, cover the top with rice once again and pour the remaining melted ghee.

Cover the dish and place inside a pre-heated oven at 300°C for about 10-15 minutes. Serve hot. Do not mix. Serve from one side right to the bottom, so that you get both the layers of the biryani on your plate.

Serves: 6

Ande ke Pakwaan

Bharwa Ande ke Pyaaz
STUFFED ONION WITH EGGS

This is a side dish and can be served with a soup and bread and butter or even as a starter.

6 large onions, steamed
Salt to taste
1 teaspoon red chilli powder
2 tablespoons milk
6 teaspoons grated cheese

3 eggs, beaten
Dash of pepper
2 tablespoon mushrooms, canned
1 tablespoon butter

Scoop out the inside of the onions with a potato peeler carefully. Keep aside. Make scrambled eggs, with salt and pepper, chilli powder, mushrooms, milk and butter in a non-stick frying pan.

Fill the hollow onions with the scrambled eggs. Sprinkle a teaspoon of cheese on each onion. Put the onions on a baking tray. Put them under the broiler for about 5 minutes until the cheese melts. Take them out and serve hot.

Serves: 6

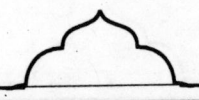

Ande ke Pakwaan

Ande aur Paalak ka Saalan
EGG AND SPINACH CURRY

This dish can be prepared a day in advance as it tastes better then! It should be served with a rice pullao. It is a green coloured dish, so serve with a yellow coloured pullao.

6 hard boiled eggs
3 tablespoons oil
1 teaspoon garam masala mixture, whole
2 onions grated
8 cloves of garlic, whole
1 teaspoon turmeric powder
2 teaspoons coriander powder
$1/2$ cup yogurt, beaten
1 tablespoon lemon juice (to be added just before serving)

1 cup spinach boiled
Salt to taste

1 tablespoon ginger root, grated
$1/2$ cup hot water
1 teaspoon red chilli powder
1 teaspoon garam masala powder
2 tomatoes, chopped

Peel the boiled eggs and keep aside. Drain the spinach and puree in a blender, and keep aside.

Heat oil in a pan, add the garam masala mixture and onions at once. Be careful as it will splatter. Add the ginger and garlic and stir fry for about 5-7 minutes. Add the hot water and simmer for another 5 minutes. Add all the spices, yogurt, tomatoes and salt and simmer for about 5 minutes. Then add the pureed spinach and whole boiled eggs and heat through. Add lemon juice just before serving.

Note: Do not use silver spoon or dish to serve eggs as it will get stained.

Serves: 6

Ande ke Pakwaan

Anda Mattar Curry
EGG AND PEAS CURRY

This is eaten with boiled rice. It can also be served with a dry potato curry, papadums, a coriander chutney and a yogurt raita. Can be served for lunch or dinner.

6 eggs, hard boiled	1 cup peas
3 tablespoons oil	
1 teaspoon garam masala mixture, whole	
2 onions, grated	1 tablespoon ginger root, grated
8 cloves of garlic, whole	½ cup hot water
2 tablespoons tomato puree	1 teaspoon turmeric powder
1 teaspoon red chilli powder	2 tablespoon coriander powder
1 teaspoon cumin powder	1 teaspoon garam masala powder
Salt to taste	1 cup hot water

Peel the boiled eggs and wash them in cold water. Keep aside. Boil the peas in 2 cups of water along with a pinch of salt and a teaspoon of sugar, when boiled, drain and keep aside.

Heat oil in a pan. Add the garam masala mixture. At once, add the onions and cover as the oil will splatter. Stir fry for a minute and add the ginger, garlic and hot water and simmer for about 5 minutes.

Add all the spices and cook for about 5 more minutes. Then add the additional hot water to make the gravy. Simmer for about 5-10 minutes, then drop in the eggs, and the drained, boiled peas and mix well.

Serve with rice.

Serves: 6

Ande ke Pakwaan

Ande ke Kofte
EGG BALLS IN GRAVY

This egg curry tastes good with a pea pullao. It is good for lunch and dinner.

6 eggs, hard boiled	1 cup mashed potatoes
Salt to taste	1 teaspoon lemon juice
1 teaspoon cumin seeds	1 teaspoon chilli powder

For the batter

6 tablespoons besan	$1/4$ cup water approx.
1 teaspoon baking powder	1 cup oil for frying

For the gravy

3 tablespoons oil	1 teaspoon garam masala mixture
2 large onions, grated	1 tablespoon ginger root, grated
8 cloves of garlic, crushed	$1/2$ cup hot water
2 tablespoons tomato puree	1 teaspoon turmeric powder
1 teaspoon chilli powder	2 teaspoons coriander powder
1 teaspoon garam masala powder	Salt to taste
1 cup hot water	

A few coriander or mint leaves, chopped (for garnish)

Peel the eggs and cut them into halves, keep aside. Put the mashed potatoes in a bowl and mix lemon juice, cumin and chilli powder. Divide the potato mixture into 12 equal portions. Place one piece of halved egg inside one portion of mashed potatoes and form into a small ball.

Make a batter with besan, water and baking powder. Dip each potato and egg ball into the besan batter and deep fry in hot oil in a wok. Drain the koftas on a paper towel.

To make the gravy, first heat oil in a pan. Add the garam masala mixture. Put in grated onions and fry. Add ginger, garlic and hot water. Simmer for about 5 minutes. Add the tomato puree and all the spices, salt and hot water. Simmer for about 10 minutes.

Put the fried egg koftas in a serving bowl and pour the gravy on top. Sprinkle on top with coriander or mint leaves.

Serve hot with rice.

Serves: 6

Ande ke Pakwaan

Katori ke Ande
BAKED EGGS IN BOWLS

This dish can be served with bread and butter sandwiches for brunch, a late night T.V. supper, or as a first course.

6 'Katoris'	6 teaspoons oil, to grease the bowls
6 eggs	Salt to taste
1 teaspoon red chilli powder	6 tablespoons milk
6 teaspoons butter	6 teaspoons grated cheese

Take 6 bowls and grease them with a teaspoon of oil each. Break one egg in each bowl. Sprinkle salt and all the other ingredients equally into each bowl. Do not mix. Put the bowls on an oven tray and bake them at 300°C. for about 10-15 minutes. Check the eggs to see if they are cooked. Remove them from the oven and serve them placed in individual plates.

Serves: 6

Tarkaariyan
—Vegetables—

Tarkaariyan

Vegetables are an essential constituent of a healthy diet. More and more people are becoming vegetarian. In India, fresh vegetables are brought in everyday in the vegetable market called 'mandi'. There is a lot of activity in all towns, as there is a 'mandi' in every town, during the early hours. Truck loads of vegetables and fruits are unloaded. The vegetables are sold at a retail price here and one can get a good bargain.

Vegetables are so versatile in our Indian cooking and can be curried in many different ways. There are a number of sweets and deserts made from vegetables, the recipes for which you will find in this book.

Tarkaariyan

Aloo ka Saag
POTATO CURRY

'Aloo' is such a versatile vegetable, that it can be curried, mashed, fried, boiled, baked, made into paranthas and even cooked with rice.

2 tablespoons 'ghee'
2 onions, ground
2 teaspoon red chillies, ground
2 teaspoons coriander powder, mixed with 4 teaspoons water
1 teaspoon turmeric powder, mixed with 2 teaspoons water
6 medium sized potatoes, peeled and cubed
2 cups water
Few leaves of green coriander, chopped

1 teaspoon cumin seeds
12 cloves of garlic, ground
Salt to taste

3 tomatoes, chopped

Heat ghee in a pan and add the cumin seeds. When they turn brown, add the ground onions. Fry the onions till golden brown then add the garlic paste and the spices paste along with salt. Cook for about 10 minutes until the ghee floats on top.

Add the potatoes, water and tomatoes and stir them well. Keep covered for about 20 more minutes, until the potatoes are tender. Sprinkle the coriander leaves prior to serving. This tastes good with hot buttered chappatis or with boiled rice.

Serves: 6

Tarkaariyan

Karahi wale Aaloo
POTATOES COOKED IN A WOK

This is a crispy and dry dish. It tastes good with 'puris'. It is good to carry on picnics or good for a packed lunch as it does not spill.

3 tablespoons of oil	1 teaspoon cumin seeds
1/2 teaspoon mustard	1 onion, sliced
5 cloves of garlic, sliced	1 teaspoon ginger root, sliced or grated
6 medium potatoes, peeled and cubed	1 teaspoon turmeric powder
1 teaspoon red chilli powder	2 teaspoons coriander powder
Salt to taste	2 cups water (approx.)
1 teaspoon mango powder or 1 teaspoon lemon juice	
1 teaspoon garam masala powder	

Heat oil in karahi. Add the cumin and mustard seeds and stir for about half a minute. Add the onions and stir for another 5 minutes, then add the garlic and ginger root and mix. Add the potatoes and stir fry for about 10-15 minutes. Then add all the spices and salt. Sprinkle a little water and cover with a lid for about 5 minutes. Open the lid and put the rest of the water and stir fry. Cover again and simmer on very low flame. When potatoes are cooked and the water is absorbed mix in the mango powder or lemon juice and garam masala powder. Turn off the flame and keep covered until ready to serve. All the liquid should have dried and the oil should be visible among the potatoes.

Serves: 6

Tarkaariyan

Aloo Hariyali
GREEN POTATO CURRY

2 tablespoons ghee or oil
2 onions, grated
5 cloves of garlic, ground
2 green chillies, seeded and ground
1/2 teaspoon red chilli powder
Salt to taste
1 tablespoon lemon juice
1/2 cup coriander leaves or mint leaves, ground
6 medium potatoes, boiled, peeled and cubed
A few green coriander leaves, for garnish

1 teaspoon cumin seeds
1/2 cup water
2 teaspoons ginger root, grated
1/2 teaspoon turmeric powder
2 teaspoons coriander powder
1 cup hot water
1 teaspoon garam masala powder

Heat oil in a pan and add the cumin seeds. When the seeds are brown add the ground onions and stir fry for about 10 minutes. Add water and simmer for about 2 more minutes. Then add garlic, ginger root and ground green coriander paste. Stir fry for about 5 minutes. Add rest of the spices along with salt and cook for about 5 minutes, stirring all the time. Put in the potatoes and hot water and mix well, cook on very low heat for 10 minutes. Add the lemon juice and garam masala powder and keep the lid on. Turn off flame. Pour into a serving dish and garnish with green coriander on top.

Serve with hot chappatis or rice.

Serves: 6

Tarkaariyan

Dibbe Ki Sabzi
TIFFIN VEGETABLE OR POTATO, CAULIFLOWER AND PEAS VEGETABLE

This is a very popular vegetable combination often served in most homes for brunch, along with hot buttered chappatis.

3 tablespoons oil
2 onions, chopped
8 cloves of garlic, chopped
4 potatoes (medium) peeled and cut lengthwise
1 small cauliflower, cut into flowerets (soak in salted hot water for 1 hour)
1 cup green peas, shelled
1 teaspoon red chilli powder
Salt to taste
3 tomatoes, chopped
A small bunch of coriander leaves, chopped
2 teaspoons roasted cumin seed powder
1 teaspoon cumin seeds
1 tablespoon ginger root, sliced
1 tablespoon lemon juice
1 teaspoon turmeric powder
2 teaspoons coriander powder
1 green chilli, sliced
1 cup hot water

Heat oil in a wok, add the cumin seeds. Stir fry the onions, ginger root and garlic for about 5 minutes. Then add the potatoes and stir fry for another 5 minutes. Add the cauliflower and peas and mix well. Cover and cook for about 10 minutes, and stir at least twice. Add all the spices, salt and mix. Then add the tomatoes and the hot water and cover and simmer on a low flame for about 10-15 minutes. When the vegetables are cooked, add the coriander, cumin powder and the lemon juice. Mix well. Turn off the flame and keep the lid closed until ready to serve. Serve the vegetable dish with hot buttered chappatis, yogurt, coriander chutney and 'churri' salad.

Serves: 6

Tarkaariyan

Paalak Paneer Kofta Curry
SPINACH AND CHEESE BALL CURRY

This is a rich sort of curry with a spinach sauce. It is very popular in most restaurants. Order it with a 'pea pullao' or with a roti. The dumplings are made of potatoes and cottage cheese, simmered gently in a thick curried spinach puree.

For the dumplings
2 medium potatoes, peeled and boiled
1 tablespoon raisins
1 tablespoon unfried cashewnuts, broken
Salt to taste
1 tablespoon onion, chopped finely
1 green chilli, chopped finely
½ cup water
¼ lb. paneer, crumbled
1 tablespoon lemon juice
1 tablespoon coriander leaves, chopped
3 tablespoons self-raising flour
1 cup oil, for frying

For the spinach gravy
1 bunch of fresh spinach (1 cup frozen spinach can be used)
A pinch of salt
2 onions, ground or grated
1 teaspoon garam masala mixture, whole
8 cloves of garlic, ground
1 tablespoon ginger root, ground or grated
1 cup hot water
3 tomatoes, chopped
1 teaspoon red chilli powder
Salt to taste
3 tablespoons oil
2 cups water
1 tablespoon lemon juice
1 teaspoon turmeric powder
2 teaspoons coriander powder
1 teaspoon garam masala powder
2 tablespoons beaten yogurt, for garnish

To make dumplings: Mash the potatoes in a bowl and set aside. In another bowl, mash the crumbled paneer and mix the raisins and the cashewnuts, along with salt, lemon juice, onion, coriander leaves and green chilli. Mix well with your hands.

Make a batter in a separate bowl with flour and water and keep aside. Divide the mashed potatoes into 6 equal portions. Take one portion and form like a cup. Fill the hollow centre with the spicy paneer mixture and gently close the opening. Form into a neat ball. Make all the balls in the same manner. Dip each ball into the flour batter and drop into the hot oil in a wok. Fry the koftas and drain them out and keep aside.

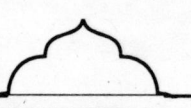

Tarkaariyan

To make the spinach gravy: Wash the spinach leaves and boil in water and salt for about 15 minutes. Drain, cool and puree. Keep aside.

Heat oil in a pan, add the whole garam masala mixture. After half a minute add the onions, ginger and garlic and stir fry for about 5 minutes. Add the hot water and simmer for another 5 minutes. Add the tomatoes, salt, and spices, spinach puree, garam masala powder, lemon juice and water mix well and simmer for about 5 minutes. Turn off the flame and keep it covered.

Arrange the koftas on a serving platter. When ready to serve, pour the hot spinach puree sauce over the dumplings. Serve at once, do not stir. Pour the yogurt on top as garnish.

Serves: 6

Subz Kebab
VEGETABLES KEBAB

This excellent barbecue dish can be prepared in advance but can be barbecued at the time of eating. It tastes good with 'naan'.

6 large bell peppers (capsicum)
1 teaspoon cumin seeds
1 teaspoon ginger root, grated
1 teaspoon turmeric powder
2 teaspoons coriander powder
2 tablespoons lemon juice
1/2 cup potatoes, boiled, peeled and mashed
1/4 cup peas, boiled
2 tablespoons oil
1 onion, chopped finely
3 tomatoes, chopped
1 teaspoon cumin powder
Salt to taste
1 teaspoon red chilli powder
1/4 cup split yellow moong dal, boiled
1 tablespoon melted ghee with 1 teaspoon of ground garlic paste.

Cut the tail end of the bell pepper and scoop the insides out. Wash under running water. Heat oil in a pan, stir fry the cumin seeds and the onions. Add ginger root and tomatoes and simmer for 5 minutes. Add all the spices and salt and cook for another 5 minutes. Add the rest of the ingredients and mix well. Divide the vegetable mixture into 6 equal portions. Stuff each bell pepper with this mixture and pack it firmly. Baste the garlic ghee around each bell pepper. Barbecue the peppers on a charcoal barbecue or under the broiler. Turn them over and baste some more garlic ghee on top.

Serves: 6

Tarkaariyan

Paneer ka Soola
CHEESE SHISH OR SHASHLIK KEBABS

This is a barbecued dish made from paneer. It is easy to make and a good substitute for a non-vegetarian barbecue. Paneer can be made at home (see p.14) or bought from the grocery shops.

2 tablespoons mango or mixed pickle, oil drained out
1 lb. of paneer, cut into 2 inch cubes
1 tablespoon Tandoori Masala (commercially sold)
1 cup natural yogurt, tie it and drip it for 1 hour in a wet muslin cloth
Salt to taste   1 teaspoon garam masala powder
2 green chillies, sliced, for garnish
1 onion, cut into rings and soaked in 1 tablespoon of lemon juice, salt and 1 teaspoon roasted cumin powder, for garnishing.

Put the 2 inch paneer pieces on a large plate. Make a small slit on one side and stuff in some pickle inside. Wrap a bit of white thread around the paneer piece to hold the pickle inside. Treat every paneer piece the same way.
In a glass bowl, put yogurt, tandoori masala, salt and garam masala powder and mix it well. Marinate the paneer pieces in the yogurt for about an hour.
Place the paneer pieces on a baking sheet, and put it under the broiler for about 5 minutes on each side.
Otherwise, thread the paneer sulaas on skewers and cook on a charcoal fire. The either method can be applied.
Shift the paneer pieces on a large platter. Cover them with onion rings soaked in lemon juice and spices and also scatter the sliced green chillies on top. Serve hot.

Serves: 6

Tarkaariyan

Matar Paneer
PEAS AND INDIAN CHEESE CURRY

This is a very popular dish in most restaurants.

1 cup fresh peas (canned can also be used)
1 teaspoon sugar
½ lb. paneer (see p.14)
3 tablespoons oil
2 onions, ground
1 teaspoon ginger root, ground
2 tablespoons tomato puree
1 teaspoon red chilli powder
Salt to taste

1 teaspoon 'garam masala' powder
½ cup oil, for frying
1 teaspoon cumin seed
8 cloves of garlic, ground
1 cup hot water
1 teaspoon turmeric powder
2 teaspoons coriander powder

Boil peas with sugar. Drain them when boiled and keep aside.

Cut the paneer into one inch square cubes. Heat oil in a wok and deep fry the paneer, a few at a time. When a light golden brown, drain them on a paper towel and keep aside.

Heat oil in a pan, add the cumin seeds. Add the ground onions, garlic and ginger and stir fry for about 5 minutes. Add the ½ cup hot water and simmer for another 5 minutes. Add the tomato puree and stir in all the spices and the salt. Add the remaining hot water and simmer for about 5-10 minutes

Lastly add the fried paneer, boiled peas and the garam masala powder. Simmer for about 5 minutes and turn off the flame. Keep covered until ready to serve.

Serves: 6

Tarkaariyan

Dhingri Mattar
MUSHROOM AND PEAS CURRY

12 fresh mushrooms, sliced
1 teaspoon sugar
1 teaspoon cumin seeds
8 cloves of garlic, ground
2 tablespoons tomato puree
1 tablespoon coriander powder
1 teaspoon garam masala powder
A few coriander leaves, for garnishing

1 cup fresh green peas, shelled
3 tablespoons oil
2 onions, grated
1 cup hot water
1 teaspoon red chilli powder
Salt to taste
1 tablespoon lemon juice

Soak the mushrooms in a bowl of water and keep aside.

Boil the peas with sugar in a pan of water, when boiled, drain and keep aside.

Heat oil in a pan, add the cumin seeds, onions, ginger and garlic and stir fry for about 5 minutes. Add $1/2$ cup hot water. Simmer for about 5 more minutes then add tomato puree, spices and salt. Add the garam masala powder, mushrooms, and the remaining hot water and simmer gently for about 5-10 minutes until the mushrooms are tender. Add the peas and lemon juice and mix well. Turn off the flame and keep covered until time to serve.

Pour into a vegetable dish and garnish with coriander leaves. Serve with hot buttered chappatis.

Serves: 6

Tarkaariyan

Pudina Baigan
MINTY AUBERGINES

This is an improvised dish and tastes really good with hot buttered chappatis.

3 aubergines
1 teaspoon cumin seeds
$\frac{1}{2}$ cup mint leaves, ground (with salt and sugar to taste)
1 tablespoon ginger root, grated
1 cup hot water
1 teaspoon turmeric powder
2 teaspoons coriander powder
1 teaspoon cumin powder
Salt to taste
A few leaves of mint, to garnish

4 tablespoons oil
2 large onions, chopped finely
6 cloves of garlic, ground
1 tablespoon tomato puree
1 teaspoon red chilli powder
1 teaspoon mango powder
1 teaspoon garam masala powder
2 teaspoons brown sugar

Wash the aubergines and make about 6 to 8 slits with a knife all around them. Carefully, insert the ground mint into the incisions and roll the aubergines in the leftover ground mint.

Heat oil in a wok, add the cumin seeds and the onions. Stir fry for about 5 minutes. Add the ginger, garlic, $\frac{1}{2}$ cup hot water and the aubergines with the rest of the spices and salt. Cover and simmer for about 15 minutes. Turn the aubergines over add the brown sugar, and some more hot water and stir. Cover and cook for another 10 minutes. By now, the aubergines should be tender. Occasional hot water is added to soften the aubergines. The gravy should be very thick.

Put the aubergines curry onto a serving platter and sprinkle the mint leaves on top.

Serve with boiled rice or hot chappatis and a bowl of yogurt.

Serves: 6

Tarkaariyan

Mirch ka Saalan
BELL PEPPER CURRY

This is sweet, sour and hot curry. It is served with rice 'biryanis'. Most Muslims prepare this dish on the festival of 'Idd'. I have simplified the recipe.

6 bell peppers	3 tablespoons oil
1 teaspoon cumin seeds	2 onions, ground
1 tablespoon ginger root, ground	5 cloves of garlic, ground
1/2 cup hot water	1 teaspoon turmeric powder
1 teaspoon coriander powder	1 teaspoon cumin powder
1 teaspoon garam masala powder	Salt to taste
1/2 cup tamarind water	2 tablespoons brown sugar
1/4 cup roasted peanuts, ground with a little water	

Cut the bell peppers into quarters or halves. Clean them from inside and wash and keep aside.

Heat oil in a wok and put cumin seeds. At once add the onions, ginger and garlic pastes and stir fry for about 5 minutes. Add the hot water and the bell peppers and simmer for about 5-10 minutes. Add the remaining ingredients to the bell peppers and simmer on a low flame for about 10 more minutes. When the gravy thickens turn off the flame and keep covered until time to serve.

Serves: 6

Tarkaariyan

Baigan ka Bharta
MASHED EGGPLANT

This is a delicious way of eating eggplants as most kids in India do not like this vegetable! This is a unique way to prepare this dish, so before starting to cook this dish, you must have 1 live charcoal ready! (optional). So here goes....

3 eggplants, roasted on the gas flame until black
2 tablespoons oil
2 large onions, chopped finely
1 teaspoon red chilli powder
2 large tomatoes, chopped finely
3 teaspoons lemon juice
2 tablespoons coriander leaves, chopped

1 teaspoon cumin seeds
2 green chillies, chopped
2 teaspoons coriander powder
Salt to taste
1 teaspoon roasted cumin seed powder

For the garnish
1 peel of an onion, washed
1 teaspoon 'ghee'

1 live charcoal

After roasting the eggplants on the gas flame or under the broiler, peel the eggplants. Mash them with a fork, in a bowl and discard the tails and the peels, and keep aside.

Heat oil in a pan, add the cumin seeds.

Add at once the onions and the green chillies. Stir fry for about 2 minutes. Add all the spices, tomatoes and salt. Simmer for about 5 minutes. Add the mashed eggplants, lemon juice, cumin powder and the coriander. Stir. Take off fire.

Put the onion peel on top of the mashed eggplants and place the charcoal on top of the onion peel. Pour the ghee on top of the live charcoal. Immediately shut the pan with a lid. The smoke of the ghee on the charcoal will flavour the eggplant 'bharta'. We call this process 'dhua' or 'dhoni'.

Open the lid after 5 minutes and discard the onion peel and the charcoal! Serve the 'baigan bharta' on a serving dish with hot buttered chappati.

Serves: 6

Tarkaariyan

Meethe Tamatar
SWEET TOMATOES

2 tablespoons oil
1 lb. tomatoes, chopped
1 teaspoon red chilli powder
Salt to taste
2 tablespoons brown sugar

1 teaspoon cumin seeds
1 teaspoon turmeric powder
1 teaspoon cumin powder
1 tablespoon malt vinegar

Heat oil in a pan and add the cumin seeds. Add the tomatoes at once and stir fry. Add all the ingredients and mix. Cover and cook on a low flame for about 15 minutes until the tomatoes get cooked. Eat with hot chappatis or buttered bread.

Serves: 6

Kola ka Saag
PUMPKIN CURRY

2 tablespoons oil
1 teaspoon cumin seeds
In a bowl mix: $1/2$ cup water, with 1 teaspoon chilli powder
1 teaspoon turmeric powder
2 green chillies, chopped
Salt to taste
2 teaspoons sugar

$1/2$ teaspoon fenugreek seeds

2 teaspoons coriander powder
1 lb. of pumpkin, peeled and cubed
2 teaspoons mango powder
2 cups hot water

Heat oil in a wok and add the fenugreek seeds and cumin seeds. Pour in the spice mixture from the bowl and let it simmer for about 5-10 minutes, on a low flame. Add the green chillies and the rest of the ingredients. Mix well. Cover and cook for about 15-20 minutes, until the 'kola' is tender. It will be a watery vegetable. Dish it out in individual bowls and eat it with hot puris!

Note that no garlic and onion is used in this dish.

Serves: 6

Tarkaariyan

Sabut Bhindi
WHOLE CURRIED OKRA

Always wash okra before cutting, otherwise it gets gluey! Wash and pat dry the okra with a paper towel before cutting.

1 lb. okra	3 tablespoons oil
1 teaspoon cumin seeds	2 onions, chopped
1 teaspoon ginger root, grated	10 cloves of garlic, chopped
1 teaspoon turmeric powder	1 teaspoon red chilli powder
2 teaspoons coriander powder	Salt to taste
1 teaspoon mango powder	1 teaspoon cumin powder
1 teaspoon garam masala powder	2 tomatoes, chopped

A few green coriander leaves, for garnishing

Cut the heads and tails of the okra and make a long slit lengthwise on one side of the okra, without separating it. Heat oil in a wok and add the cumin seeds. After half a minute, add the onions, ginger root and garlic and stir fry for about 5 minutes. Add okra and stir fry for about 10-15 minutes. Add all the spices along with the tomatoes and mix well. Cover with a lid and simmer for about 15-20 minutes more. Stir occasionally so that the okra does not stick to the bottom. When tender, turn off the flame. Keep covered until ready to serve. Garnish the dish with coriander leaves on top. Serve hot with chappatis.

Serves: 6

Tarkaariyan

Khatte Chole
SOUR CHICKPEAS

This dish tastes good with 'puris'.

3 teaspoons oil
½ cup onions, grated
½ teaspoon garam masala mixture, whole
½ cup hot water
2 tablespoons tomato puree
1 teaspoon cumin powder
Salt to taste
2 cups chickpeas, soaked overnight and boiled in tea leaves
2 teaspoons garam masala powder

1 teaspoon cumin seeds
1 tablespoon ginger root, grated or sliced
1 teaspoon red chilli powder
2 teaspoons coriander powder
1 teaspoon mango powder

For the garnish
1 onion, cut in rings
4 green chillies, sliced lengthwise
1 lemon quartered
1 potato, boiled, peeled and cut in round thick slices

Heat oil in a wok. Add the cumin seeds and the garam masala mixture. After a minute, add the onions and ginger and stir fry for about 5 minutes. Add the hot water, tomato puree, spices and salt. Add the chickpeas. Mix them with a spoon and add the mango powder and garam masala powder. Stir fry for about 5 minutes until all the liquid has been absorbed.

Put the 'cholas' in a serving dish and garnish with onions rings, green chillies, lemon and potato slices.

Serve with hot 'puris' and 'halwa'.

Serves: 6

Tarkaariyan

Tawa Chana
GRIDDLE GARBANZOS

This is a fast food dish but can also be eaten as part of the main meal. It is eaten with a bun called 'pau' or with a fried bread called 'Bhatura'. It is a typical dish from the state of Punjab. A lot of small fast food shops called the 'Dhabaas' make it on a large iron griddle called the 'Tawa'.

3 tablespoons oil	1 teaspoon cumin seeds
2 onions, sliced	
2 cups chanas, (garbanzos) boiled or canned	
1 teaspoon red chilli powder	1 teaspoon garam masala powder
1 teaspoon cumin powder	Salt to taste
1 teaspoon ginger root, sliced	1 green chilli, sliced
1 teaspoon mango powder	1 tablespoon lemon juice
1 onion, sliced (for garnish)	2 green chillies, sliced (for garnish)
A small bunch of coriander leaves, chopped	
1 potato, boiled, peeled, cubed (for garnish)	

Heat oil on the tawa and put the cumin seeds. Stir fry the onions for about a minute. Add the chanas add all the spices and stir fry for about 5 minutes. Add lemon juice and mix. Put the 'chanas' on a platter and garnish with the raw onion slices, green chillies, coriander leaves and potato cubes.

Serves: 6

Tarkaariyan

Achaari Gobhi
CAULIFLOWER CURRY IN PICKLE SPICES

This is a traditional dish of the North. It tastes good with hot buttered thick chappatis and a bowl of cool yogurt.

3 tablespoons oil
1/2 teaspoon mustard seeds
1/2 teaspoon nigella or onion seeds
1 teaspoon turmeric powder
1 teaspoon coriander seeds, crushed
Salt to taste
1 teaspoon mango powder
1/2 teaspoon cumin seeds
1/2 teaspoon aniseeds
1 big cauliflower, cut into flowerets
1 teaspoon dried red chillies, crushed
5 cloves of garlic crushed
1/2 cup hot water
1 tablespoon oil from any pickle

Heat oil in a wok. Add all the seeds. Meanwhile keep the cauliflower soaked in a bowl of hot salted water for about 10 minutes. Drain the cauliflower and put the flowerets into the wok and stir fry for about 10 minutes. Add all the spices, salt and hot water. Cover for about 5 minutes. Stir it and add the mango powder and the oil from any pickle. This will give it a real pickle flavour! Take it off and keep covered until ready to serve.

Serves: 6

Kaande ka Saag
ONION CURRY

2 tablespoons oil
1 lb. onions, sliced thickly
2 teaspoons red chilli powder
Salt to taste
2 cups hot water
1 teaspoon cumin seeds
1 teaspoon turmeric powder
2 teaspoons coriander powder
1 tablespoon mango powder

Heat oil in a pan. Add the cumin seeds, after a minute add the onions and stir fry. Add all the spices and mix and then add the hot water and simmer for about 20 minutes until the onions wilt and are tender. Remove and serve with chappatis.

Serves: 6

Tarkaariyan

Punjabi Karhi
CHICKPEA FLOUR AND YOGURT CURRY

This 'Karhi' is very popular in Punjab. It is eaten with hot buttered chappatis or tandoori 'rotis'. In most parts of India, karhi is called and eaten as 'Karhi chaawal' a twin dish with rice. The flavour and taste varies from house to house. Pakoras are fried and added to the Karhi. A story goes that one should always make karhi with pakoras as one must not separate the mother (karhi) from her children (pakoras)!

For the Pakoras
1 teaspoon cumin seeds
Salt to taste
1 teaspoon garam masala powder
$1/3$ cup water approx.

For the Karhi
1 cup yogurt
Salt to taste
1 teaspoon red chilli powder
2 green chillies, sliced

For the baghar
$1/2$ teaspoon cumin seeds
$1/2$ teaspoon mustard seeds
4 small dried red chillies

1 cup besan (chickpea flour)
1 onion, chopped
1 teaspoon red chilli powder
1 teaspoon baking powder
1 cup oil, for frying

$1/2$ cup besan, sieved
1 onion, sliced
1 teaspoon turmeric powder
4 cups water

1 tablespoon oil
$1/2$ teaspoon fenugreek seeds
4 cloves of garlic, sliced
A pinch of asafoetida (heeng)

To make the pakoras, sieve the 'besan' into a bowl. Add all the ingredients and mix with water to make a thick paste. Heat oil in a wok and deep fry a spoonful of batter, which form dumplings. Fry about 5 at a time. Drain and keep aside.

To make the karhi, put the yogurt in a large pan. Add 'besan', all the ingredients and mix well with your hands, until no lumps are left. Now add water and mix with a spoon. Put the pan on the stove and cook it for about 20-25 minutes until it thickens. After about 10 minutes, you must start stirring it constantly as it will boil over and spill. Stirring also prevents the karhi from clogging. When ready turn off the heat. Add the pakoras to the karhi.

Make a 'baghaar' by heating oil in a frying pan. Add all the ingredients. Keep shaking the pan. After about 1 minute, pour this over the karhi.

Serve the karhi in a deep bowl and provide 'Katoris' (small bowls) for every person to eat from. Serve with chappatis or boiled rice.

Serves: 6

Tarkaariyan

Sindhi Karhi
CHICKPEA FLOUR IN TAMARIND CURRY

This is another kind of karhi made by the Sindhi community of India.

2 tablespoons oil	1 teaspoon cumin seeds
1/2 teaspoon fenugreek seeds	A pinch of asafoetida
2 teaspoons ginger root, chopped	2 green chillies, chopped
2 dried red chillies, broken in pieces	1/2 cup besan (chickpea flour)
1/2 cup tamarind water or juice	10 curry leaves
4 cups of water	1 potato, peeled and cubed
2 carrots, peeled and sliced	1 egg plant, cubed
20 french beans, cut into four	2 drumsticks, cut and boiled (optional)
1 horseradish, peeled and sliced (Optional)	
2 tomatoes, chopped	Salt to taste
1 tablespoon jaggery or brown sugar	
A few leaves of coriander leaves, chopped	

Heat oil in a large pan. Add the cumin, fenugreek, asafoetida, ginger root, green and red chillies. After a minute add the besan and stir fry. Remove from the heat after about 2 minutes. Add the tamarind water and all the ingredients except jaggery and coriander leaves. Return the pan to the stove and cook for about 20-25 minutes on a low flame. Simmer until all the vegetables are tender. Keep stirring. Taste for the salt and add accordingly. Add the jaggery or brown sugar and let it boil once. Pour into a deep bowl and sprinkle the coriander leaves on top.
Serve with boiled rice and fried papadums and a 'churri' salad.

Serves: 6

Dal ke Pakwaan
—Lentils—

Dal ke Pakwaan

Dal is rich in protein and is very essential in a vegetarian diet, daily. Dals can be made in either as a dry curry or a soupy curry. It is served in the North with chappatis and is often referred as 'Dal roti' and in the South it is eaten with rice—Dal chaawal. It is almost the first solid which is given to babies when first weaning them. A dal and rice soft khichree is prepared with salt and ghee or butter and fed to the babies. Some dals are easily digested except the chana dal. Dal is bought by the Indian housewife in bulk for the month's supply. All the different kinds are bought, cleaned and then stored in glass jars. Dals or lentils can be used in many ways. They can be curried, made into sprouts, powdered, ground, made into sweets, and even used in making dosas and idlis. Various recipes are given to make the different types of dals. Most dals are now sold in grocery department stores and also in health food shops. It is a good accompaniment with rice and is a great dish to serve at curry lunches.

Kaale chane

Aaloo matar sabzi

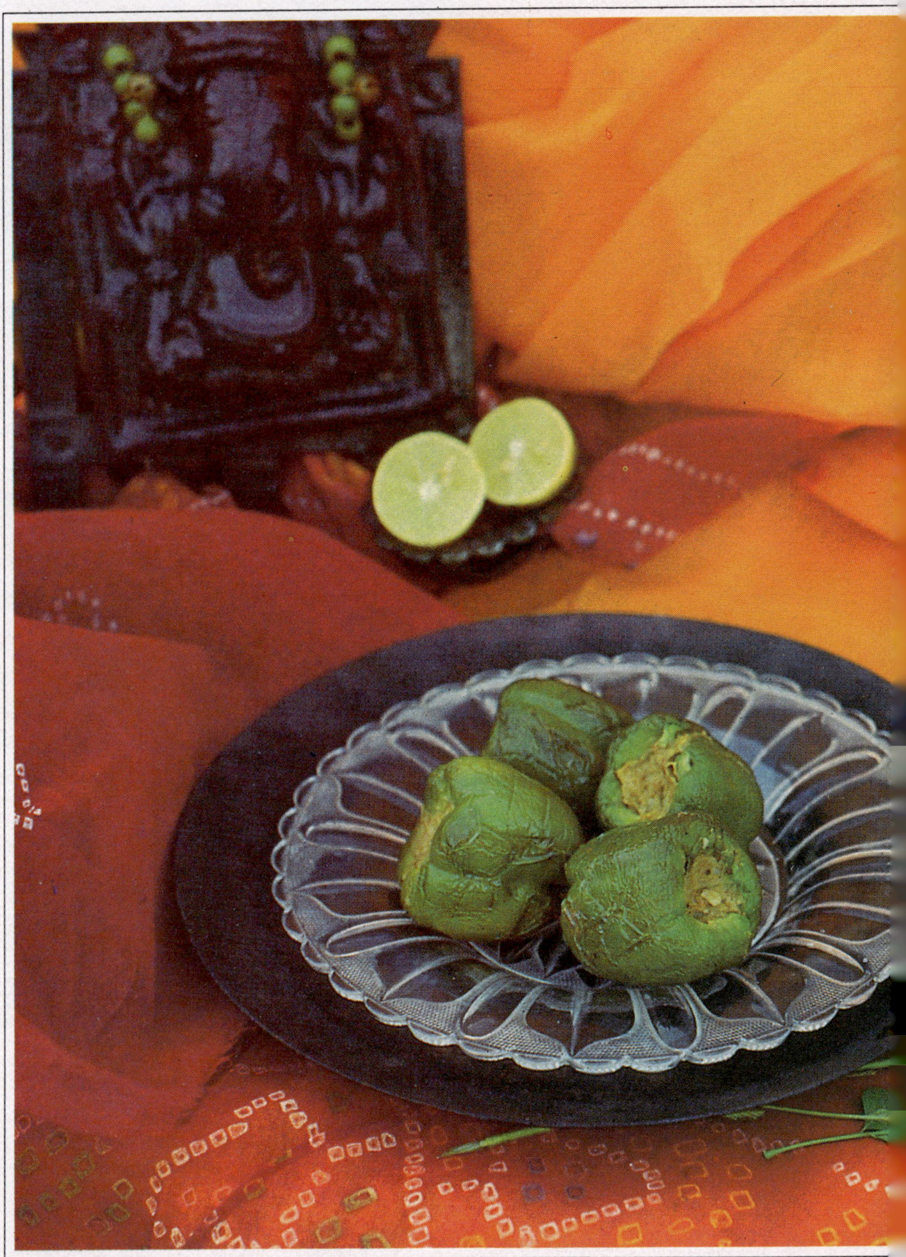

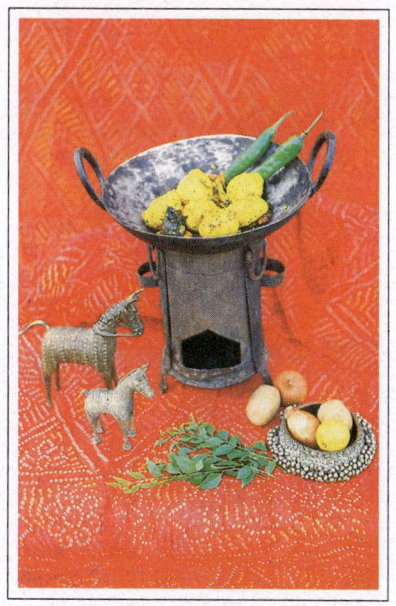

Kadai aaloo

Stuffed shimla mirch

Naan, tandoori roti & chole

Dal parantha (Korma ki roti)

Dal ke Pakwaan

The different types of lentils are:

Chana dal—Yellow split chickpea
This dal is very important, as it can be cooked as a dal with spices, or with a vegetable in the dry form. 'Besan' flour is made by grinding this dal into a powder form.

Malka Masoor dal—Pink lentil dal
This dal is available all around the world in 1 lb. packages. It is pink in colour, but turns a yellow hue after cooking. The dal requires the least cooking time.

Masoor Sabut — Black lentils
This is the whole masoor dal; after splitting this, the outer black grayish cover is discarded and the pinkish lentils are revealed. It is good to make a thick curry with white rice.

Mung dal—(Dhuli Hui)
Split yellow mung beans
This is a yellow coloured dal and is easily digested. It is called 'Dhuli hui' mung dal which means washed mung dal. It is mostly used as a dal curry or cooked together with rice as a soft khichree.

Mung dal—(Chilke waali)
This is a green coloured dal. The mung dal is split into two and the green cover is still fixed on the dal. It is healthy to eat this as the skin is still on the dal. It tastes best with hot buttered chappatis.

Mung dal (Sabut)
This is the whole mung bean dal. It is used in making bean sprouts. Can also be used in cooking it as a dal or as a mung bean dal khichree. It is full of proteins.

Tuwar dal—Yellow split dal
It is also called pigeon peas in English. It is cooked with vegetables and tamarind to make the famous 'Sambhar' south Indian dal curry. Lemon, green mangoes, tamarind or dried mango powder is used to flavour this dal. It tastes best with boiled rice.

Urad dal (Dhuli Hui)—Split black gram dal.
This is used in making dosas and idlis, specialities from the south. It can also be made into a dal curry. This dal has a sticky texture. It is not so easy to digest, so one must not eat too much of it. Because of its sticky texture, it is good for making dal vadaas or dahi bhallas.

Urad dal (Sabut)
This is the whole black gram dal. This is used mostly in Punjab to cook their famous 'Maah di daal'. It is cooked with spices and a lot of butter or ghee is poured just before eating it. It is cooked like a thick dal.

Dal ke Pakwaan

Subzi Waali Dal
DAL WITH VEGETABLES

This is a complete meal if served with boiled rice or hot buttered chappatis. It is a nutritious dish also, as a lot of vegetables are boiled together with the dal. It is easy to prepare.

1 cup split yellow mung dal
1 teaspoon turmeric powder
1 carrot, peeled and cubed
3 tomatoes, chopped
$1/4$ cup fresh mint, chopped
2 onions, sliced

For the baghaar
1 tablespoon ghee
4 cloves of garlic, sliced
1 teaspoon coriander powder

For garnish
1 tablespoon lemon juice (to squeeze on top)
1 onion, sliced and fried
A few coriander leaves, chopped for garnish

4 cups water
1 large potato, peeled and cubed
12 french beans, sliced
1 aubergine, chopped
Salt to taste

1 teaspoon cumin seeds
1 teaspoon red chilli powder

    Clean the dal and wash it several times in a sieve under a cold water tap. Soak it for about 2 hours.

    Put the dal and the water in which it has been soaked (4 cups) in the pressure cooker or a large pan. Add all the ingredients and vegetables. Cook for 15 minutes in the pressure cooker or 25-35 minutes in the pan. If cooking in a pan make sure that dal and vegetables are cooked. Pour in a serving dish.

    Make a 'baghaar' to pour on top of the dal. Heat 'ghee' in a frying pan. Add the cumin seeds and garlic. Let the cumin seeds get brown. Take off the pan from the stove and quickly put the chilli and coriander powders. Stir it once and pour the contents of the frying pan on top of the dal in the dish. Do not stir. Lastly, pour the lemon juice on top and garnish with the fried onions and coriander leaves.

Serves: 6

Dal ke Pakwaan

Sambhar
SOUTH INDIAN LENTIL CURRY

Sambhar is a must in South India in their daily meals. It is made from Tuwar dal and a combination of various vegetables. It is eaten with boiled rice, dosa or idli. It has a special flavour with the addition of sambhar powder. Sambhar powder can be made at home or bought commercially. Always store it in the fridge as it will remain fresh.

1 cup tuwar dal (pigeon pea)	4 cups water
1 tablespoon sambhar powder	1 teaspoon turmeric powder
$1/2$ cup tamarind water	1 eggplant, cubed
2 carrots, peeled and cubed	12 french beans, sliced
1 large potato, cubed	8 small button onions, peeled
2 tomatoes, chopped	Salt to taste
2 green chillies, cut into half	

For the baghaar

2 tablespoons oil	1 teaspoon mustard seeds
1 teaspoon chana dal or urad dal	Few curry leaves
2 dried red chillies, crumbled	2 clove of garlic, sliced

Wash the tuwar dal. Put the dal in a large pan. Add water and all the ingredients. Simmer on medium heat for about 25-30 minutes. Stir a few times. When the dal is cooked along with the vegetables, turn off the stove.

For the baghaar, heat oil in a pan and put all the ingredients in the hot oil. After half a minute, pour the contents into the sambhar. Mix.

Serve the sambhar in a large deep bowl with a big ladle. Tastes good with boiled rice and papadums.

Serves: 6

Dal ke Pakwaan

Tuwar Dal Tarke Waali
PIGEON PEA DAL TEMPERED WITH TARKA

This is a tasty dal, and most homes all over India eat it. Of course, the method of cooking varies in all homes.

1 cup tuwar dal	4 cups water
Salt to taste	1 teaspoon turmeric powder
6 dried 'amchoor' pieces (dried green mangoes, sold in shops)	

For the Tarka

1 tablespoon ghee	1 teaspoon cumin seeds
2 whole dried red chillies	4 cloves of garlic, sliced

Wash the dal. Put the dal and the other ingredients in a pressure cooker for 15 minutes. When cooked, open and stir. Put in a serving dish.

For the 'tarka' heat the ghee and add the cumin, red chillies and garlic. After half a minute, pour the 'tarka' over the dal. Do not stir.

Serve it hot, with boiled rice, fried papadums, a coriander chutney and yogurt.

Serves: 6

Dal ke Pakwaan

Meethi Gujrati Dal
SWEET DAL FROM GUJARAT

This is a speciality of Gujarat. It is best eaten with boiled rice, fried papadums and pickle. It is sweet in taste but delicious.

1 cup tuwar dal	4 cups of water
1 teaspoon turmeric powder	1 teaspoon red chilli powder
1 teaspoon coriander powder	Salt to taste
$1/2$ cup tamarind water	1 tablespoon jaggery or brown sugar

For the 'baghaar'

1 tablespoon ghee	1 teaspoon mustard seeds
10 curry leaves	

Clean and wash the dal. Put it in a pressure cooker along with all the ingredients. Cook for about 15-20 minutes. Open and stir well. Pour into a serving dish

Heat ghee to make the baghaar. Add the mustard seeds and curry leaves in the ghee. After half a minute, pour this over the dal and stir it in. Serve the dal hot with rice.

Note that no onion and garlic has been used in the preparation.

Serves: 6

Dal ke Pakwaan

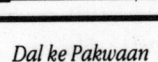

Malka Masoor Matar Waali
MASOOR DAL WITH PEAS

This is the dal which cooks very fast, even without a pressure cooker! Since this dal is available easily in all grocery stores, it is easy to store.

1 cup masoor dal (pink lentils)	4 cups water
1 cup frozen peas	1 teaspoon turmeric powder
1 teaspoon red chilli powder	2 teaspoons coriander powder
Salt to taste	1 teaspoon garam masala

1 tablespoon lemon juice (to be added after the dal is cooked)

For the baghaar

1 tablespoon oil or ghee	1 teaspoon cumin seeds
4 cloves of garlic, sliced	

Clean and wash the dal. Put the dal in a deep pan with all the ingredients. Mix well. Cook on the stove for about 25-30 minutes, stirring most of the time. When cooked, add the lemon juice.

Make a 'baghaar' by heating the oil or ghee. Add the cumin and garlic and after half a minute pour it over the dal. Serve with boiled rice and fried papadums, 'raita' and pickle.

Serves: 6

Dal ke Pakwaan

Mung Dal Malai Waali
MUNG DAL WITH CREAM

This is special dal, good for serving at parties. It is a 'mughlai' speciality. It tastes good with hot 'puris'. It is rich in calories too!

1 cup yellow split mung dal	3 cups of water
1 cup of yogurt	1 teaspoon green chillies, ground
1 tablespoon coriander leaves, ground	1 tablespoon ginger root, ground
8 cloves of garlic, ground	1 large onion, ground
1 tablespoon of ghee or butter	Salt to taste

$\frac{1}{2}$ cup 'malai' or fresh cream (to be added when dal is cooked)
1 teaspoon garam masala powder

For the 'tarka' or baghaar

1 tablespoon ghee	2 bay leaves
1 teaspoon garam masala mixture, whole	12 sliced almonds
Few coriander leaves (for garnish)	One leaf of silver varak

Clean the dal and wash it several times. Put the dal with water and all the other ingredients in a deep pan, except the cream. Simmer on a medium flame, uncovered, for about 25-30 minutes. When the dal is cooking keep on stirring occasionally. When the dal is cooked pour into a silver or party dish, stir in the malai.

Make the 'tarka' by heating the ghee. Add the whole garam masala mixture, almonds and bay leaves. After a minute, pour this over the prepared dal. Do not stir. Sprinkle coriander leaves on top. Lastly put the silver varak on top. Serve hot.

Serves: 6

Dal ke Pakwaan

Dal Hariyali
DAL WITH GREEN SPICES

This dal is green in colour after cooking, as most of the spices are green in colour. It is good to serve with a pea pullao, fried papadums, coriander chutney and a glass of salty 'lassi'.

1 cup green split mung dal	4 cups of water
2 tablespoons mint leaves, ground	1 teaspoon green chillies, ground
1/4 cup spinach leaves, ground	Salt to taste
2 onions, ground	6 cloves of garlic, ground
1 tablespoon ginger root, grated	1 teaspoon 'garam masala' powder
1 teaspoon lemon juice	

For the 'tarka'

1 tablespoon ghee	1 teaspoon cumin seeds
2 cloves of garlic, chopped	1 green chilli, chopped
A spring of mint, for garnish	

Clean and wash the dal. Put the dal in the pressure cooker with water and all the ingredients, for about 15 minutes and if cooking in a deep pan, then for about 25-35 minutes. When the dal is cooked, pour in a serving dish.

Make the 'tarka' by heating the ghee in a small frying pan. Add the cumin, garlic and green chilli to the ghee. After half a minute pour it over the prepared dal. Do not stir. Garnish with a spring of mint on top, before serving.

Serve hot.

Serves: 6

Dal ke Pakwaan

Rajasthani Gaadi Dal with Khaand
THICK MUNG DAL WITH SUGAR

1 cup yellow split mung dal	2 ½ cups of water
1 teaspoon turmeric powder	Salt to taste
1 teaspoon roasted cumin seed, powder	3 tablespoons melted hot ghee
2 tablespoons 'Khaand' (sugar)	

Wash and clean the dal. Put it in a deep pan alongwith water, turmeric and salt. Cook it for about 30 minutes or until the dal is cooked dry. Stir it occasionally.

When ready pour it into a serving dish. Sprinkle the roasted cumin seed powder on top. Make a well in the centre of the dal. Pour hot melted ghee inside the small well. Then pour the sugar on top of the ghee. Serve it with buttered boiled rice. Eat it hot as the ghee will thicken otherwise. Khichree is also eaten the same way in Rajasthan!

Serves: 6

Dal ke Pakwaan

Chana Dal Lauki Waali
CHICKPEA DAL WITH WHITE PUMPKIN

This dish may be eaten with hot, buttered chappatis and a coriander chutney. It is cooked with 'lauki' (white pumpkin). It is a thick dry dal curry.

1 cup chana dal	1 cup 'lauki', peeled and cubed or grated
4 cups water	1 teaspoon turmeric powder
1 teaspoon red chilli powder	2 teaspoons coriander powder
1 tablespoon ginger root, slices	8 cloves of garlic, whole
Salt to taste	1 tablespoon 'garam masala' powder

1 tablespoon lemon juice (to be added when dal is cooked)
1 tablespoon roasted cumin seeds (to be added when dal is cooked)

For the 'baghaar'

2 tablespoons ghee	1 teaspoon cumin seeds
1 onion, sliced	A few mint leaves, for garnish

Clean and wash the dal. Put the dal with the lauki and all the other ingredients except lemon juice and roasted cumin seeds, in the pressure cooker for 15-20 minutes.

When the dal is cooked, pour it into a serving dish, mix the lemon juice. Make the 'baghaar' by heating the ghee. Add the cumin seeds and the onions. Let the onions get cooked for about 5 minutes to a deep brown. Pour this over the prepared dal. Do not stir. Garnish on top with chopped mint leaves—serve hot.

Serves: 6

Dal ke Pakwaan

Dal Makhani
BUTTER DAL

This dal is a popular dish in most restaurants. It is very tasty and is eaten with hot tandoori 'Rotis'. Even though the basic ingredients remain the same, it tastes different in every restaurant.

1 cup green mung split dal	$1/2$ cup split urad dal
4 cups water	1 onion, sliced
1 tablespoon ginger root, sliced	1 teaspoon turmeric powder
1 teaspoon red chilli powder	1 teaspoon coriander powder
1 teaspoon garam masala powder	Salt to taste

For the 'tarka'

2 tablespoons butter	1 teaspoon cumin seeds
5 cloves of garlic, sliced	2 green chillies, sliced (for garnish)
Few green coriander leaves (for garnish)	1 lemon quartered (for garnish)

Wash the green mung dal and urad dal in cold water after cleaning. Wash several times.

Put the dals together with water and all the other ingredients in the pressure cooker for about 15-18 minutes. Otherwise in a deep pan for about 30-40 minutes. When cooked it should be thick. Give it a stir and pour out into a deep serving dish.

Make the tarka (seasoning) to pour over the prepared dal. Heat butter in a frying pan, add the cumin seeds and garlic at once. After a minute pour this tarka over the dal. Do not stir. Sprinkle green chillies on top befor serving.

Serves: 6

Dal ke Pakwaan

Punjabi Maah Sabat
WHOLE URAD DAL

This dal is a speciality of Punjab. It has now become the favourite dal of most 'Dhaabaas' (roadside restaurants) of North India. It is relished with 'Tandoori Rotis' with lots of butter poured on top, alongwith a horseradish and onion salad.

1 cup sabut urad dal	4 cups water
1 tablespoon ginger-root, sliced	6 cloves of garlic, crushed
2 onions, chopped	2 green chillies, chopped
Salt to taste	$1/2$ cup yogurt
1 teaspoon red chilli powder	1 teaspoon coriander powder
1 teaspoon garam masala powder	2 tablespoons ghee

For the 'tarka'

2 tablespoons ghee or butter	1 teaspoon cumin seeds
2 cloves of garlic, sliced	

Accompaniments

$1/4$ cup melted ghee or butter	2 lemons, cut into halves
4 whole green chillies	1 raw onion, sliced
1 glass of yogurt 'Lassi' drink	A stack of 'Tandoori', Rotis!

Clean and pick the urad dal. Wash several times in water under a cold water tap.

Put the dal in the pressure cooker with water and all the other ingredients. Mix it once and cook for about 15-20 minutes. Open and stir it. It should be of a thick consistency and the dal should be completely blended in the water like a thick soup. If you are cooking in an ordinary pan, you have to cook for at least an hour or so and may have to keep on adding about 2 more cups of hot water as this dal takes longer to cook. You must keep stirring most of the time and keep on mashing the dal on the side of the pan, as you keep stirring.

Pour the cooked 'Maah dal' in a large ceramic dish. Make a 'tarka' to pour on top. Heat the ghee or butter and add the cumin and garlic. After a minute, pour this over the dal in the dish.

Serve with accompaniments—a star hemp woven bed to sit on. Wear a sarong or lungi to get the atmosphere right.

Serves: 6

Bhaartiya Rotis
—Indian Breads—

Bhaartiya Rotis

Bread is eaten in many forms in India. It is fried, baked, grilled and barbecued. Here are a collection of various methods to make the Indian breads and 'Rotis'. Roti is made on an iron griddle called the 'Tawa' or it can be fried (puri) in a karahi (wok). We also make our bread in a clay oven called the tandoor. Breads are also stuffed with paneer or different vegetables and spices.

Bhaartiya Rotis

Phulka
BASIC BREAD WITHOUT GHEE

This 'phulka' is usually eaten at both mealtimes and sometimes in the form of a parantha for breakfast.

1 $\frac{1}{2}$ cups whole wheat flour
$\frac{1}{2}$ cup water to mix (approx.)

Salt to taste
$\frac{1}{2}$ cup plain flour, for rolling out

Sift the flour in a bowl. Mix salt and pour the water and knead with your hand.

If the water is not enough, an additional 2 tablespoons of water may be added. Make a soft dough. Divide it into 12 equal balls. Roll out each ball with a rolling pin on a floured board about 5 inches in diametre.

Heat the iron griddle (tawa) on a medium flame. Put the rolled out phulka on the hot tawa. When small bubbles start to appear quickly flip it over. Cook on the other side for the same time. Remove the tawa with a pair of tongs and put the first roasted side onto the direct flame. Watch and behold, it will puff up like a balloon full of air!

Serve it at once, or make all and stack them in the chappati box. Keep them warm.

Yields: 12

Bhaartiya Rotis

Chappatis
INDIAN BREAD WITH GHEE

This is basically the same as the 'Phulka', but is buttered on one side with melted ghee. It tastes good with a dal or a vegetable with gravy.

1 cup whole wheat flour
Salt to taste
$1/2$ cup plain flour, for rolling

1 cup plain flour
$1/2$ cup water to knead (approx.)
$1/2$ cup ghee, melted

Sift the flours together in a bowl. Add the salt. Knead it with water into a soft dough. Divide into 12 equal balls. Roll out each ball on a floured board into a 6 inch round disc.

Heat the iron griddle (tawa) on a medium flame. Put a rolled out disc on the tawa for a minute. To test, see that the disc moves easily on the tawa. Turn it over and cook the second side. Remove the tawa with a pair of kitchen tongs and put the first side of the cooked chappati on the naked flame. It will puff up like a balloon! Remove it at once and put in a chappati box on a napkin. Put a teaspoon of ghee all over one side of the hot chappati. Serve hot or make all 12 of them and keep warm.

Note: If you have an electric cooking range, then you can dab the chappati with a folded napkin, and it will rise slightly and cook through.

Yields: 12

Bhaartiya Rotis

Puris
FRIED BREAD

These are very quick to make. They are normally made at festivals, weddings, parties for a large gathering of people, as they are made fast. These can be eaten hot or cold, but hot ones are preferred. Any cooking oil can be used to fry the 'puris'.

1 cup plain flour	1 cup whole wheat flour
Salt to taste	1 tablespoon oil
$1/2$ cup oil, for frying	

Sieve both the flours together. Add salt, oil and make it into a stiff dough by adding water. Divide into 20 equal sized balls.

Roll out each ball of dough on a greased board. Heat oil in a wok. When it is very hot, fry each puri in the oil. Press the puri down and release it several times with a slotted cooking spoon, so that it rises quickly. It will again puff up like a balloon. Turn it over fast and after a split second, take it out with a slotted spoon. Drain the puris in a bowl with a paper towel. Serve hot with a dry or curried potato dish.

Note: Different flavoured puris can be made in the same way with the desired flavour, e.g. mint chutney, coriander chutney, cumin seeds, chilli powder, etc. can be added!

Yields: 20

Bhaartiya Rotis

Tandoori Roti
BREAD COOKED IN A CLAY OVEN

This tandoori roti is very popular in Delhi and Punjab. Most people have a 'tandoor' clay oven built in their homes. These are quick to prepare and taste good with dal, lots of butter and yogurt and a dry vegetable. It is baked inside a tandoor or clay oven sunk in the ground, with live charcoal.

2 cups whole wheat flour
$1/2$ cup water to mix (approx.)
$1/4$ cup ghee, melted

Salt to taste
$1/2$ cup plain flour, to roll in

Sift the flour and add salt, in a bowl. Pour water and mix into a soft dough.

Divide the dough into 8 equal parts. Roll out on a floured board into thick round discs about 6 inches in diametre. Put water on one side of the rolled out disc and stick it to the walls of the tandoor if you have one.

Otherwise put the wet side on a cookie sheet in an oven marked 375°C for about 7-10 minutes. Broil for a minute the top side and put ghee on one side. You can serve without putting ghee also as some people like the crispy hot rotis that way.

Note: Curried mashed potatoes can be mixed with the dough or any other desired flavour can be added.

Yields: 8

Bhaartiya Rotis

Tawa Paranthas
GRIDDLE FRIED BREAD

These are made the same way as the chappatis but are fried on the tawa with melted ghee or butter. It is a very common dish at breakfast in many homes, to eat with an omelette! It is also carried in a packed lunch with a dry vegetable or as a stuffed vegetable 'parantha'. Paranthas are normally triangular or square in shape, whatever shape you like.

2 cups whole wheat flour
1/2 cup water to mix (approx.)
1/2 cup ghee or butter, melted

Salt to taste
1/2 cup plain flour, to roll in

In a bowl, sift the flour and add salt. Add water to make a soft dough. Divide the dough into 10 equal balls. Roll out each ball on a floured board about 3 inches. Brush some ghee on one side of the disc. Fold in half, brush ghee again over the folded half. Then fold once again. It will form a triangle. Roll it gently into a 5 inch triangle parantha.

Heat the tawa (griddle) and put the parantha on the hot tawa. Cook on one side and pour a tablespoon of ghee on the top and smear it all over the surface. Turn it over and put ghee all over this side also. Turn it once more so that the ghee gets cooked on both sides. You have to be quick in flipping it over. Remove from the tawa and stack them on a paper towel in the chappati box.

Serve hot.

Yields: 10

Bharwa Paneer Parantha
STUFFED PANEER BREAD

This bread is a meal in itself. A lot of things can be stuffed in this parantha, e.g. dry curried potatoes, mashed vegetable, paneer, mint chutney, mashed curried peas, cauliflower, horseradish, etc. The paranthas are usually eaten with natural yogurt. In Punjab this is their daily bread.

2 cups whole wheat flour
1 tablespoon ghee
½ cup plain flour, to roll
For the Paneer stuffing
1 cup paneer, crumbled
1 teaspoon cumin powder
1 tablespoon green coriander leaves, chopped
1 teaspoon garam masala powder
2 green chillies, chopped
1 teaspoon lemon juice

Salt to taste
½ cup water to mix (approx.)
½ cup ghee, for frying

Salt to taste

1 onion, chopped
1 teaspoon cumin seeds

Sift the flour and salt in a bowl. Mix the ghee in the flour and add water to make into a soft dough. Keep aside.

Mix the paneer with all the ingredients, and use this as the stuffing.

Divide the dough into 12 equal balls. Roll out 2 discs on a floured board. Place a spoonful of stuffing on top of one rolled out disc and flatten it with your hands. Place the other disc over the stuffing and seal the edges. Roll out lightly. The discs should be about 5 inches in diametre.

Heat the tawa and put the double stuffed paneer parantha on it. Pour ghee over and around the parantha and turn it after a minute. Apply ghee over the other side and cook on both the sides. When crispy brown, take it off. Repeat until all are made. Serve hot.

Yields: 6

Batia
THICK BREAD

'Batias' are a thick chappati with lots of ghee and sometimes flavours like a coriander chutney put inside the dough along with some spices.

2 cups whole wheat flour	4 tablespoons ghee
1 teaspoon cumin seeds	1 teaspoon red chilli powder
Salt to taste	1 small onion, chopped
1 green chilli, chopped	$\frac{1}{2}$ cup water to mix (approx.)
$\frac{1}{2}$ cup plain flour, to roll in	$\frac{1}{4}$ cup ghee, to put on top

Sift the flour in a bowl. Rub in the ghee. Add the other ingredients and mix with water. Divide the dough into 8 equal parts.

Roll out each ball on a floured board, about 3 inches in diameter. Heat a 'Tawa' and cook the batia on one side for a minute. Turn the batia over and cook the other side, until it is cooked. Turn it again 2 or 3 times and keep on roasting it on both the sides until it is crispy. Take it off.

Put the 'batia' on a board. Pour a tablespoon of melted ghee over one side of the 'batia' and make incisions with a spoon several times, so that the ghee drains inside the 'batia'. Serve at once. It will break very easily as it is like a thick flaky bread. Eat with a chilli chutney or a vegetable and raita.

Yields: 8

Bhaartiya Rotis

Baati
BREAD BALLS

These are made in Rajasthan on picnics or weddings, when a lot of bread is required. They are baked in ashes of the clay stoves or toasted in the ashes of cow dung cakes! But we can make it in our ovens. Baatis are eaten with dal and it is a twin dish called 'Dal Baati'.

2 cups whole wheat flour
Salt to taste
$1/4$ cup milk
1 cup curried mashed potatoes

$1/2$ cup ghee, melted
$1/4$ cup yogurt
$1/4$ cup water (if necessary)

Sift the flour in a bowl. Rub in the ghee, add the salt and mix with yogurt and milk. Make into a stiff dough. Divide the dough into equal parts.

Fill each ball with a spoonful of curried potatoes. Close firmly and bake them in an oven marked 350°C for about 20-30 minutes. Turn them once or twice until they are baked and cooked. Serve them with melted butter. As you eat them dip each one in the bowl of melted butter before putting it in your plate.

Can also be served and eaten with a dal.

Yields: 8

Bhaartiya Rotis

Khurmi Naan
SPICY UNLEAVENED BREAD

This is a special bread and very light and delicious. Eat with a yogurt salad and vegetable kababs.

2 cups plain flour
1 teaspoon baking powder
1 egg
2 tablespoons ghee, melted
2 tablespoons milk (approx.)

Salt to taste
1 teaspoon bicarbonate of soda
2 teaspoons sugar
2 tablespoons natural yogurt

For the stuffing
6 cloves of garlic, ground
2 tomatoes, chopped

2 green chillies, chopped

For the topping
2 tablespoons of oil

1 tablespoon poppy seeds

Sift the flour in a bowl. Add the salt, baking powder, soda, egg, sugar, ghee, yogurt and mix with milk. Form into a soft dough. Cover the bowl with a damp muslin and keep in a warm dark place for about 3 hours.

Take it out and knead again. Mix the garlic, chillies and tomatoes in the dough. Knead well. Divide into 8 equal portions on a floured board.

Heat a tawa. Roll out each ball into an oval 4 inches shape. Put one 'naan' at a time on the tawa. Cook for about 1 minute. Remove from the tawa (griddle) and keep aside. Cook all the naans in the same way. Place all the cooked naans on a cookie sheet. Brush the uncooked side with the melted ghee and sprinkle some poppy seeds on top of all. Put them under the broiler for about 1 or 2 minutes, until they rise. Remove and serve hot.

Note: Paneer can be mixed instead of the garlic mixture, to make a paneer naan. A plain naan can be made without any stuffing.

Yields: 8

Bhaartiya Rotis

Podina Bhatura
MINTY FRIED BREAD

This is served with chana (garbanzoes) or a potato curry. It can be made plain or spicy.

2 cups self raising flour
Salt to taste
1 egg
2 tablespoons ghee, melted
2 tablespoons dried mint

1 teaspoon bicarbonate of soda
2 tablespoons sugar
$1/2$ cup yogurt
$1/2$ cup water (approx.) to mix
2 cups oil for frying

Sift the flour in a bowl. Add all the ingredients except the mint and oil for frying. Make into a soft dough. Cover with a damp muslin and keep in a dark place for about 3 hours, to rise. Knead once again. Mix the dried mint and knead again. Divide into 8 equal balls.

Roll out each ball on a greased board about 4 inches in diameter.

Heat the oil in a wok and fry one bhatura at a time. Turn it over and fry on both sides. Drain on a paper towel. Serve hot.

Yields: 8

Chaawal ke Pakwaan
—Rice Dishes—

Chaawal ke Pakwaan

Rice is the staple food in most parts of India. It is an important cereal. It adds vitamins and carbohydrates to the diet. The Hindi name for rice is 'chaawal'. There are many kinds of rice, but the best quality is the Basmati rice, grown in Kashmir. Basmati rice is available all over the world. It is very light and long grained. As a substitute the long grain Patna rice may also be used.

The simplest way to cook rice is: Measure 1 cup of rice. Wash it well and put 2 cups of water and boil in a pan till the water evaporates leaving the rice soft and separate.

Rice can be made in so many different ways. Boiled, pullaos, biryanis, puddings, dosas, idlis, and many other variations.

Chaawal ke Pakwaan

Saade Chaawal
PLAIN BOILED RICE

This is the basic method to cook rice. It can be made into several flavours later on, if desired.

2 cups rice
1 teaspoon salt
4 cups water

Wash the rice several times. Put rice, water and salt and cook uncovered for about 15-20 minutes. Turn off the flame and cover. Let it sit on the stove until time to serve. It tastes good with dal, a curry 'rasam', sambhar, yogurt or any other spicy curry.

Serves: 6

Khichree
KEDGEREE

Khichree is a combination of rice and dal cooked in water in a soft consistency. It is generally fed to babies as it is easy to digest. It can also be made by adding some vegetables. It can be served with yogurt, papadums, a coriander chutney and pickle.

2 cups rice
Salt to taste
5 cups water
1 teaspoon cumin seeds
$1/2$ cup yellow split mung dal
1 teaspoon turmeric powder
1 tablespoon ghee

Wash rice and dal together. Put them in a pan with salt, turmeric and water and mix well. Heat ghee in another pan, and temper with cumin. Pour it over the rice and dal mixture and stir in it. Put the pan on the stove and cook it on medium heat for about 25-30 minutes until the rice and dal are cooked and well blended. Additional hot water may be added if you want the khichree to be soft.

Serve it on a big platter with lots of melted ghee in the centre of the khichree. You can even eat it with some 'boora' (powdered sugar).

Serves: 6

Chaawal ke Pakwaan

Makhani Chaawal
BUTTERED RICE

This is a delicately flavoured rice. It goes well with any curry or even karhi (besan flour curry) and is good to serve guests also.

2 cups Basmati rice	4 cups water
Salt to taste	2 tablespoons butter
1 teaspoon 'shahi zeera' (black cumin)	12 cashewnuts, fried for garnishing

Wash the rice several times in water. Put rice, water and salt in a rice cooker. Cook uncovered. After 10 minutes, heat the butter in a small frying pan and add the 'shahi zeera' to the butter. After a minute, pour it over the rice. Stir with a fork and mix it. When the rice is cooked, serve on a platter and sprinkle the fried cashewnuts on top.

Serves: 6

Matar Pullao
PEA PULLAO

This dish can be eaten without any accompaniments and also with any curry or yoghurt and pickle.

2 tablespoons oil or ghee
2 bay leaves
2 cups basmati rice
4 cups water
1 teaspoon garam masala mixture, whole
1 onion, sliced and fried dark and crisp for garnishing
Salt to taste
1 onion, sliced
1 cup green peas, frozen, fresh or canned

Heat oil and add the garam masala mixture alongwith bay leaves. Add the onion and stir fry for about 5 minutes. Add the rice and peas. Stir for a minute and add the water and salt. Cook for about 20-25 minutes stirring occasionally. Turn off the heat. Cover and do not open till serving. It can also be cooked in a rice cooker. Serve on a rice platter, sprinkle some crispy fried onions on top.

Serves: 6

Chaawal ke Pakwaan

Gatte ka Pullao
CHICKPEA FLOUR DUMPLINGS RICE

This is a special rice dish from Rajasthan. It is made of rice and thick chickpea flour dumplings. It is delicious to eat with any vegetable curry and fried papadums along with a coriander chatni.

To make gattas

1 teaspoon cumin seeds
Salt to taste
$1/2$ teaspoon red chilli powder
$1/3$ cup buttermilk or water to mix

1 cup besan (chickpea flour)
2 cups water to boil in
1 tablespoon oil
1 teaspoon tumeric powder

For the rice

2 cups basmati rice
3 tablespoons oil
1 teaspoon whole garam masala mixture
3 bay leaves
10 cloves of garlic, ground
2 teaspoons red chilli powder
1 onion, sliced and fried crisp, for garnishing
$1/2$ cup coriander leaves, chopped, for garnishing

4 cups water
Salt to taste

1 onion, sliced
1 teaspoon turmeric powder
2 tablespoons lemon juice

Make the 'gattas' by sifting the besan flour into a bowl. Add cumin, salt, oil, chilli powder, turmeric and work into a soft dough with either buttermilk or water. Divide the dough into 6 parts. Roll each part on a greased board to form long snake like shapes, about 4 inches long. Boil water in a pan, when it starts boiling slowly put in all the 6 besan pieces. Boil for about 10-15 minutes until the 'gattas' are cooked. Take them out with a fork and cut each one into 1 inch long piece. Keep aside. The boiled water can be used in any vegetable curry to make a tasty gravy.

Wash the rice and soak in water for about half an hour. Heat oil and add the whole garam masala mixture and bay leaves. Add onions and stir fry for about 5 minutes. Add garlic paste and all the spices, lemon juice and salt, stir. Lastly add the rice and water and mix. Let it cook either in the rice cooker or the original pan for about 20 minutes. Add the boiled 'gattas' and mix in the rice with a fork gently. Cover and simmer for another 10-15 minutes until all the water has absorbed and the rice is tender. Turn off the flame. Keep covered until time to serve. Put on a rice platter. Sprinkle the fried onions on top and garnish with coriander leaves.

Serves: 6

Chaawal ke Pakwaan

Baigan ka Pullao
AUBERGINE RICE

This rice is a good variation from the common rice recipes.

1 medium aubergine	½ cup oil, for frying
3 tablespoons oil	
1 teaspoon garam masala mixture, whole	
2 bay leaves	1 onion sliced
1 teaspoon ginger root, sliced	1 green chilli, sliced
1 teaspoon turmeric powder	Salt to taste
1 teaspoon red chilli powder	1 teaspoon mango powder
2 cups basmati rice	4 cups water

Few leaves of green coriander, chopped for garnishing

Cut the aubergine into cubes and deep fry the pieces in hot oil in a wok. Drain and keep aside.

Heat oil in a pan, add the garam masala mixture and bay leaves. Add the onion, ginger and green chilli and stir fry for about 5 minutes. Then add all the spices and salt and mix. Add the rice, water and the fried aubergine pieces and cook for about 20 minutes. Stir with a fork. Cover and simmer for another 10 minutes and do not open until ready to serve. Turn off the flame. Put on a plate and garnish with coriander leaves.

Serves: 6

Chaawal ke Pakwaan

Paneer Pullao
INDIAN CHEESE RICE

This is a good dish to serve at parties. It goes well with a vegetable curry, raita and fried papadums.

1 cup paneer, (see paneer recipe)	$\frac{1}{2}$ cup oil, for frying
4 tablespoons oil	2 bay leaves
4 cloves	1 teaspoon cumin seeds
1 onion, sliced	1 teaspoon turmeric powder
2 green chillies, sliced	2 cups basmati rice
4 cups water	$\frac{1}{2}$ cup green peas
Salt to taste	2 tablespoons lemon juice

1 onion, sliced and fried crisp for garnishing
12 cashewnuts, fried for garnishing

Cut the paneer into one inch cubes. Heat oil and deep fry the paneer pieces. Drain and keep aside.

Heat oil in a pan, add the bay leaves, cloves and cumin. Then add the onion and stir fry for about 5 minutes. Add the turmeric, green chillies, rice, water, peas, salt and lemon juice. Mix well. Cook for about 20 minutes uncovered, with an occasional stir. Add the fried paneer pieces and mix with a fork. Cover and cook for another 10 minutes until the rice is cooked. Turn off the flame and do not open until time to serve.

Put on a rice platter, garnish on top with fried onions and cashewnuts.

Serves: 6

Chaawal ke Pakwaan

Methi ke Chaawal
FENUGREEK RICE

This dish can be served with karhi, fried papadums and a potato vegetable.

3 tablespoons oil	1 teaspoon cumin seeds
1 onion, sliced	1 green chilli, sliced
2 cups basmati rice	4 cups water
1 tablespoon dry methi leaves (fenugreek)	
1 teaspoon red chilli powder	1 teaspoon turmeric powder
Salt to taste	

Heat oil in a pan. Add the cumin seeds. Stir fry the onions and chilli for about 5 minutes. Add the washed and cleaned rice, water, methi leaves, red chillies, turmeric and salt. Stir. Cook for about 25 minutes uncovered. Keep stirring occasionally. Cover and simmer another 5 minutes. When ready, turn off the flame and open only while serving.

Serves: 6

Chaawal ke Pakwaan

Sabut Masoor ki Biryani
BLACK LENTIL BIRYANI

This is a very tasty dish. It can be eaten by itself with just a raita and fried papadums.

For the sabut masoor dal
2 tablespoons oil
1 teaspoon garam masala mixture, whole
1 teaspoon cumin leaves
1 onion, sliced
10 cloves of garlic, whole
1 teaspoon red chilli powder
2 tomatoes, chopped
1 cup black lentils (sabut Masoor dal) cleaned and washed
4 bay leaves
1 tablespoon ginger root, grated
1 teaspoon turmeric powder
2 teaspoons coriander powder
Salt to taste
2 cups water

For the rice
2 cups basmati rice
4 cups water

For the biryani
4 tablespoons ghee, melted
1 cup yogurt with 1 teaspoon garam masala powder mixed in
$1/4$ cup hot milk with $1/2$ teaspoon saffron mixed in
$1/4$ cup lemon juice
2 onions, sliced and fried crisp
12 almonds, sliced
1 tablespoons raisins
$1/2$ cup green coriander leaves, chopped for garnishing

Heat oil in a pan. Add the garam masala mixture, bay leaves and cumin. Add the onions and stir fry for 5 minutes. Then add ginger, garlic, all the spices, tomatoes, salt and mix well. Lastly, add the black lentils and water. Let it cook for about 25-30 minutes until the dal is cooked and all the water is absorbed. Turn it off and keep aside.

Clean and wash the rice and boil it in water. When cooked, keep aside.

In a corningware glass dish, put 2 tablespoons of ghee, put a layer of rice, cover it with a layer of cooked lentils, then pour a tablespoon each of yogurt mixed with garam masala powder, milk mixed with saffron and lemon juice. Sprinkle some fried onions on top, some almonds and raisins. Cover once again with rice and repeat the process once or twice again, until all the ingredients have been consumed. The top layer should be rice. Pour the left over melted ghee on top and cover the dish. Put in an oven marked 200°C for about 15-20 minutes. Just before serving, sprinkle lots of green coriander leaves on top. Serve the rice from one side only and spoon it out right from the bottom. It will have different coloured layers. So after cooking it, enjoy your meal to satisfaction!

Serves: 6

Katori ka Chaawal
RICE BOWLS

2 tablespoons oil
1 ½ cups basmati rice
Salt to taste
For the garnish
1 tablespoon ghee, melted

1 teaspoon 'shahi zeera' (black cumin)
3 cups water
1 tablespoon raisins

6 sprigs of mint or parsley

Heat oil in a pan. Add the 'shahi zeera'. Add rice, salt and raisins. Cook uncovered for about 15 minutes. Stir with a fork. Cover and simmer another 5 minutes. Turn off the flame, let it remain on the stove. For best results, always use the rice cooker, as it turns off automatically!

Take 6 'katoris' or bowls. Grease them with the melted ghee and fill the rice in each cup. Divide the rice into 6 equal portions. Pack each 'katori' or bowl firmly and press it down. When all the bowls are packed, keep them in a warm oven.

Just before serving, take a large rice plate. Slowly, unmould the rice from one 'katori' at a time on the rice plate. Decorate each one with a sprig of mint or parsley. Serve hot, with a vegetable curry or dal and pickle.

Serves: 6

Chaawal ke Pakwaan

Bisi Bele Huliyanna
RICE AND DAL WITH VEGETABLES

It is a typical south Indian Mysore dish and is very tasty.

1½ cups rice	3 cups water
1 cup tuwar dal	2 cups water
½ cup potatoes, boiled, peeled & cubed	½ cup carrots, peeled, boiled and cubed
½ cup peas, boiled and drained	1 cup tamarind water

'Masala' Mixture

1 tablespoon oil	1 teaspoon coriander seeds
2 teaspoons chana dal	2 teaspoons urad dal
¼ teaspoon fenugreek seeds	1 tablespoon grated coconut
A pinch of asafoetida	6 dried red chillies

For the main procedure

4 tablespoons oil	1 teaspoon mustard seeds
12 curry leaves	Salt to taste
2 tablespoons ghee	
2 tablespoons cashewnuts, fried for garnishing	
A bunch of coriander leaves, chopped for garnishing	

Wash and clean the rice and dal separately and keep aside. Boil the vegetables and keep aside. Soak tamarind for about an hour, pass through a sieve and keep aside.

Next, make the 'masala' (spices) ready. Heat oil in a pan and quickly fry all the ingredients given for the masala mixture. After about 2 or 3 minutes of stir frying, grind the spices coarsely with a mortar and pestle and keep aside.

Heat oil for the main procedure. Add mustard seeds, curry leaves and tamarind water. After 5 minutes, add salt, cooked dal, boiled vegetables, masala mixture and cook for another 5 minutes, until it thickens. Add rice and ghee and mix well. Stir it briskly, all the vegetables, dal and rice should be blended well together like a soft khichree.

Put on a platter and sprinkle fried cashews and chopped coriander leaves. It is complicated to make, but tastes super!

Serves: 6

Chaawal ke Pakwaan

Tirange Chaawal
3 COLOURED RIBBON RICE

3 cups basmati rice
6 cups water
Few drops of yellow colour
1 tablespoon ghee, melted

For garnishing
1 cup salted, boiled peas
2 tomatoes, cut into rounds
1 carrot, boiled and peeled and cut in rounds

For the green coconut chutney
$\frac{1}{2}$ cup grated coconut
2 green chillies, ground
4 cup water

1 teaspoon salt
1 cup green coconut chutney
1 cup tomato ketchup

Few potato chips

1 bunch of coriander or mint leaves
Salt to taste

Grind together all the ingredients for the green coconut chutney and keep aside.

Wash the rice and boil it with salt and water in a rice cooker or an ordinary pan. When ready, keep aside. Divide the rice into 3 equal parts. Mix one part of rice with the green coconut chutney. Mix the second part of rice with yellow colour. Mix the third of rice with tomato ketchup.

Put the ghee in a rectangular Pyrex dish. Put the red layer of rice with the ketchup into the dish. Press firmly. Cover it completely with the yellow layer of rice. Press firmly. Lastly, put the green layer of rice and press firmly. Cover and put the dish in an oven marked at 200° for about 15 minutes. Just before serving slowly unmould the rice on a rice platter. Garnish with peas, chips, tomatoes and carrots. Serve with a yogurt salad.

Serves: 6

Raitas
— Yogurt Salads —

Raitas

Raitas in different combinations are extremely popular, healthy and nourishing. 'Raita' is made from yogurt and various ingredients are added to it.

Always keep in a jar some roasted cumin seed powder or seeds. They are useful whenever you make the raita.

Raita should be chilled in the fridge before serving. It is an accompaniment to a curry meal. Raitas are very cooling in the summer months. Always use a glass or a ceramic bowl to serve.

Raitas

Dahi ki Chatni
YOGURT RAITA

2 cups yogurt
1 cucumber, peeled and chopped
Salt to taste
$1/2$ teaspoon black pepper or red chilli powder
For the Baghaar
2 teaspoons oil

2 tomatoes, chopped
1 onion, chopped

1 teaspoon mustard seeds

Mix yogurt in a glass bowl. Add the tomatoes, cucumbers, onions, salt and pepper and mix well, with a spoon.

Heat oil in a pan and temper the mustard seeds for a minute. Pour this baghaar over the yogurt and mix it.

Serves: 6

Lauki ka Raita
WHITE PUMPKIN IN YOGURT SALAD

This is a very popular raita. It tastes good with a 'pea pullao' and a vegetable curry.

2 cups natural yogurt
$1/2$ cup grated lauki, boiled and drained and grated
1 tablespoon raisins
1 green chilli, chopped
1 teaspoon sugar

Salt to taste

1 teaspoon roasted cumin seed powder
$1/2$ teaspoon dried mint

Mix yogurt in a glass bowl. Add the grated 'lauki' after squeezing it tightly. Wash the raisins in a bowl of water and add to the yogurt with the rest of the ingredients. Chill for an hour before serving.

Serves: 6

Raitas

Arbi ka Raita
COCOYAM RAITA

This is a different kind of raita but very delicious. It tastes good with hot chappatis.

6 Arbis, boiled and peeled
2 cups natural yogurt
½ teaspoon red chilli powder
Few coriander leaves, for garnish
½ cup oil
Salt to taste
1 teaspoon roasted cumin seeds

Press the arbis (cocoyam) between both your palms. Heat oil in a wok. Fry each arbi till it is crisp and golden. Fry on both sides. Drain on a paper towel.

Put the yogurt in a glass bowl and add all the spices and salt. Mix the fried arbis in the yogurt. Garnish with coriander leaves and serve.

Serves: 6

Chane aur Aaloo ka Raita
CHICKPEA AND POTATO RAITA

This nutritive raita is mostly made in the North. Served usually for lunch, with chappatis or rice.

2 cups natural yogurt
Salt to taste
1 cup chickpeas or garbanzos, canned or boiled
1 teaspoon roasted cumin seed powder
1 teaspoon roasted coriander seeds, crushed
2 red chillies, roasted, crushed
1 potato, peeled and cubed
1 tablespoon tamarind water
1 teaspoon sugar

Mix the yogurt in a bowl. Add the potatoes and the chickpea along with all the other ingredients and stir. Chill before serving.

Serves: 6

Raitas

Dubble Roti ka Raita
BREAD RAITA

This is a unique raita, it tastes like a dish called 'Dahi Bara'. It can be eaten with meals or on its own at tea time.

6 slices of bread, cut into rounds
Salt to taste
1 teaspoon roasted cumin seed powder
For the chutney
$1/2$ cup tamarind water
4 cloves of garlic, crushed
1 teaspoon sugar
$1/2$ teaspoon dried mint
A few coriander leaves, for garnishing

2 cups of natural yogurt
1 teaspoon red chilli powder
1 teaspoon sugar

Salt to taste
$1/2$ teaspoon red chilli powder
1 teaspoon raisins
1 teaspoon ginger powder

Put the bread rounds in a large flat glass dish. Beat yogurt in a bowl and mix it with all the ingredients. Pour it over the bread in the dish. Make the chutney by mixing the tamarind water with all the ingredients in a separate bowl. Pour the chutney over the yogurt in the dish. Garnish with coriander leaves. Note that the chutney can also be served separately.

Serves: 6

Anannas ka Raita
PINEAPPLE RAITA

This is a sweet and sour raita. If served chilled it tastes good with a rice pullao.

3 slices of pineapple, canned
$1/2$ teaspoon salt
$1/2$ teaspoon black pepper corns, crushed fresh in the pepper mill
1 teaspoon roasted cumin seeds

2 cups natural yogurt
1 teaspoon sugar

Cut the pineapple slices into small pieces. Put the yogurt in a bowl and mix with the pineapple pieces. Add all the spices and mix. Chill before serving.

Serves: 6

Mooli ka Raita
WHITE HORSERADISH RAITA

This raita is made in the winter months when 'moolis' are in season. The 'moolis' smell a lot. Always cover the raita with a saran wrap after making it. Horseradish is rich in iodine.

1 mooli, peeled and grated
1 green chilli, chopped
1 teaspoon roasted cumin seed powder
2 cups natural yogurt
Salt to taste
Few leaves of green coriander, chopped

Put the 'mooli' and the yogurt in a glass bowl. Add all the ingredients to the bowl and mix well. Serve chilled.

Serves: 6

Matar ka Raita
PEAS RAITA

This is a tasty green pea raita. It tastes good with any pullao.

1 cup green peas, boiled or canned
Salt to taste
1 teaspoon roasted cumin seeds
1 teaspoon sugar
2 cups of natural yogurt
1 teaspoon red chilli powder
1 green spring onion, chopped

Wash the peas in cold water and keep aside. Mix the yogurt with all the ingredients and the peas together. Chill before serving.

Serves: 6

Raitas

Ankur ka Raita
MUNGBEAN SPROUTS RAITA

This is a very healthy and nutritious raita. It is good for dieters as it is a meal in itself.

1 cup mung bean sprouts	2 cups natural yogurt
Salt to taste	1 onion, chopped
1 green chilli, chopped	$1/2$ teaspoon red chilli powder
1 teaspoon sugar	1 teaspoon roasted cumin seeds
A few green coriander leaves, chopped	

Wash the mung beans sprouts in cold water and keep aside. Put the yogurt in a bowl. Add the sprouts in the yogurt with all the other ingredients and mix well. Garnish on top with coriander leaves. Chill before serving.

Serves: 6

Raitas

Karam Kalle ka Raita
CABBAGE RAITA

This fresh tasting raita is very healthy. It is full of vitamins and can be eaten with a curry, rice and fried papadums.

½ cabbage, sliced thinly
Salt to taste
1 tablespoon roasted peanuts, crushed
1 teaspoon roasted cumin seeds
Few leaves of green coriander

2 cups yogurt
1 teaspoon red chilli powder
1 teaspoon sugar
1 green chilli, chopped

Soak the shredded cabbage in a bowl of warm water with salt for about half an hour. Drain in a colander for half an hour.

Put the cabbage in a bowl with the yogurt and other ingredients. Mix well. Chill before serving.

Serve: 6

Chutneys

Chutney

Chutneys are normally freshly ground. Some can last for about a week in the fridge. 'Chatnis' are always an accompaniment with deep fried snacks and the main meal.

The most popular chutneys are made of green coriander leaves, mint, coconut, onions, green mangoes, etc.

A chutney is meant to be spicy, hot, sour and tangy. It lifts up your appetite and tingles the taste buds!

Chutney

Dhania ki Chutney
GREEN CORIANDER CHUTNEY

This is the most popular chutney. It has a fresh flavour, can be stored in a glass bottle with a lid in the fridge for about 4-5 days. It tastes well with snacks and meals.

1 cup coriander leaves, chopped
1/2 cup onions, chopped
1 tablespoon lemon juice
1/4 cup water (approx.)

3 green chillies, chopped
Salt to taste
1 teaspoon cumin seeds roasted

Wash the coriander thoroughly. Put all the ingredients in a food processor and blend to a smooth paste. The chilli can be varied according to individual preferences.

Pudine ki Chutney
MINT CHUTNEY

Mint chutney is mostly popular in the north. It is served as an accompaniment with fried snacks and main meals.

1 cup mint leaves, chopped
1 tomato
2 red dried chillies
1 teaspoon sugar

1/2 cup onions
Salt to taste
1 tablespoon lemon juice
1/4 cup water (approx.)

Soak mint leaves and wash them after an hour. Put all the ingredients in a food processor and grind to a fine paste. Store in a glass bottle with a lid.

Chutney

Lassan Chutney
GARLIC CHUTNEY

This is hot chutney which tastes good with chappatis.

20 cloves of garlic, chopped
4 dried red chillies soaked in 1 tablespoon vinegar
1 teaspoon roasted coriander seeds
Salt to taste
$1/4$ cup tamarind water
1 teaspoon roasted cumin seeds

Wash the garlic cloves and mix all the ingredients and grind on a grinding stone or in a blender.

Tamatar ki Chutney
TOMATO CHUTNEY

This chutney tastes good with dal and rice and potato chips.

5 tomatoes, blanched, peeled, chopped
1 onion, sliced, fried light brown
1 green chilli, chopped
1 tablespoon ginger root, grated
2 tablespoons vinegar
1 teaspoon roasted cumin seeds
Salt to taste
6 cloves of garlic, chopped
1 tablespoon brown sugar or jaggery

Put all the ingredients in a blender and blend to a smooth paste. Can be served with the dishes listed above.

Chutney

Churri Chutney
MIXED CHUTNEY

This chutney tastes good with dal, rice and fried papadums.

2 tomatoes	1 onion, chopped
2 green chillies, chopped	½ cup green coriander leaves
Salt to taste	1 tablespoon tamarind water or Vinegar
1 tablespoon brown sugar	½ teaspoon red chilli powder
¼ cup water	1 teaspoon roasted cumin seeds

Blanch the tomatoes in hot water and peel them. Chop the tomatoes. Put all the ingredients in a food processor and blend together. Keep in the fridge.

Lal Mirchi ki Chutney
RED CHILLI CHUTNEY

This chutney is also called the 'Gunpowder' chutney! So beware, only make it if you can eat it or else you may suffer from a Delhi belly!!

10 large dried red chillies (soaked in 1 cup water for 1 hour)
10 cloves of garlic   Salt to taste
2 tablespoons yogurt
For the baghaar
2 teaspoons oil   1 teaspoon cumin seeds

Deseed the chillies and put with water, garlic, salt and yogurt to blend into a fine paste. Take out in a bowl. Heat oil in a pan, temper the cumin seeds in oil for a minute. Pour over the chilli chutney.

Eat it with hot thick buttered 'batias'.

Chutney

Khopre ki Chutney
COCONUT CHUTNEY

This chutney is very popular to serve with snacks. It can be also used as a sandwich spread.

1 cup grated coconut, roasted dry on a pan
2 green chillies, chopped
2 onions, chopped
1/2 cup water (approx.)
Salt to taste
1 cup coriander or mint leaves, chopped
2 tablespoons lemon juice

Put all the ingredients in the blender and blend to a smooth paste. Store in the fridge.

Dosa Chutney
CHUTNEY FOR DOSA

This is a typical south Indian chutney.

1 cup fresh coconut, grated
1 tablespoon ginger root, grated
Salt to taste
1/2 cup water
For the baghaar
1 tablespoon oil
1/2 teaspoon chana dal or urad dal
5 small dried red chillies
1 cup yogurt
2 green chillies, chopped
1 tablespoon lemon juice
A few curry leaves

1 teaspoon mustard seeds
6 curry leaves

Put the coconut with all the other ingredients in the blender and grind coarsely. Put in a bowl. Heat oil in a pan and temper the mustard seeds, chana dal, curry leaves and red chillies. After a minute pour this over the ground coconut chutney in the bowl and mix. Put in the fridge.

This can be served with dosas (rice pancakes) idlis or vadai.

Chutney

Hare Aam ki Chutney
GREEN MANGO CHUTNEY

This chutney is made when the green mangoes are in season. It tastes delicious with rice and dal or with hot chappatis.

2 green mangoes, peeled, cored, diced
2 large roasted, dry red chillies
1 teaspoon roasted sesame seeds
1 tablespoon coriander seeds, roasted dry
1 green chilli, chopped
1 teaspoon roasted cumin seeds
Salt to taste
$\frac{1}{4}$ cup water (approx.)

Put all the ingredients in the blender along with the water and blend to a smooth paste. Store in the fridge.

Imli aur Adrak ki Sonth
TAMARIND AND GINGER CHUTNEY

This is a sweet and sour chutney. It can be eaten with several yogurt preparations.

4 tablespoons dried tamarind
2 teaspoons ginger powder
Salt to taste
1 teaspoon roasted cumin seeds
6 cloves of garlic, crushed
2 cups water
3 tablespoons brown sugar
1 teaspoon red chilli powder
1 teaspoon ginger root, sliced
1 tablespoon raisins

Soak the tamarind in 2 cups of water for about an hour. Strain it and mix all the ingredients except the raisins.

Cook on a medium flame, till it thickens. Add the raisins and stir for 5 more minutes. Cool and serve. Store in the fridge.

Chutney

Simla Mirch ki Chutney
BELL PEPPERS CHUTNEY

This is a cooked chutney. It is sweet and sour and can be eaten with the main meal of dal and rice.

6 cloves of garlic, chopped
1 teaspoon cumin seeds
4 tablespoon brown sugar
6 tablespoons oil
6 bell peppers, cut into 4 slices each (lengthwise)
Salt to taste

3 large red dried chillies, seeded
1 teaspoon mustard seeds
1 cup vinegar
$1/2$ cup oil, heated in a separate pan

Grind together garlic, red chillies, cumin, mustard, brown sugar with vinegar in the blender to a smooth paste. Keep aside.

Heat oil in a pan and stir fry the bell peppers for about 5 minutes. Add the ground spices and cook the spices with the bell peppers for about 10 more minutes. Add the oil and remove from the stove. Cool completely. Store in a jar.

Chutney

Kairee ki Meethi Chutney
SWEET MANGO CHUTNEY

This chutney is a great favourite of children as it tastes like curried jam! Eat it with bread, chappatis or paranthas

8 green mangoes, peeled
1 tablespoon ginger root, sliced
2 cups vinegar
12 cloves of garlic, crushed
1 cup jaggery or brown sugar
1 tablespoon raisins
3 tablespoons vinegar
1 teaspoon cumin seeds, crushed
1 teaspoon red chilli powder

Grate the mangoes. Squeeze out the excess water and keep aside in a colander.

Soak the raisins and ginger in vinegar. Put the 2 cups vinegar in a pot along with cumin, garlic and chilli powder. Boil for 5 minutes. Add the grated mangoes and jaggery and simmer on a low flame for about half an hour. Add the soaked raisins and ginger root and simmer.

Remove from the pan and pour into a dish. Cool completely overnight. Cover it at night with a cloth. Bottle it the next morning in small jars with screw top lids.

Chutney

Seb ki Chutney
APPLE CHUTNEY

This is a tasty sweet and sour chutney and can be eaten with sandwiches or chappatis.

6 green apples
2 teaspoons ginger root, sliced
2 cups water
2 tablespoons raisins
1 teaspoon red chilli powder

6 cloves
$^1/_2$ cup vinegar
1 cup sugar
12 cloves of garlic
Salt to taste

Wash and peel the apple. Cut into small cubes.

Put the apples along with all the ingredients in a thick bottomed pan and cook on a medium flame for about an hour or more. Cook it until the water is absorbed and the apple chutney thickens.

Cool completely and store in bottles.

Achaar
Pickles

Pickles add a certain ting to a curry meal. Some pickles are made at home but now with lack of time, one just rushes out and buys a bottle of pickle from the stores! But nevertheless it is always exciting and challenging to make your own pickles.

Pickles can be made in many different ways. The taste differs from region to region. The north, south, east and west regions of India have their own recipes for the pickles. Most commonly the green mango, chillies and lemon is used to make pickle. Different oils are used for different pickles

Pickles are made in the seasons whenever mangoes, lemons, cauliflower, are available in season. So look out for the month and set yourself a date with pickling time!

Achaar

Hari Mirch ka Achaar
GREEN CHILLI PICKLE

This pickle is very hot, but all chilli lovers will love it! It tastes good with dal and rice or hot chappatis and yogurt.

20 green chillies	2 teaspoons oil
1 teaspoon fenugreek seeds	1 cup oil
$\frac{1}{2}$ teaspoon asafoetida	1 teaspoon turmeric powder
2 tablespoons mustard seeds, crushed	1 tablespoon cumin seeds
$\frac{1}{2}$ cup lemon juice or vinegar	2 teaspoons salt

    Wash and dry the chillies. Cut them into halves lengthwise. Keep aside. Heat oil in a small pan and temper the fenugreek seeds. Grind the fenugreek seeds coarsely with a mortar and pestle. Keep aside.

    Heat 1 cup oil in a pan and add asafoetida. Remove from the flame and add all the spices. Cool completely. Mix the chillies and fenugreek crushed seeds in the oil. Then add the lemon juice. Keep overnight and store in bottles the next morning. Do not forget to cover at night. Can be used after 1-2 days.

Meetha Neembu ka Achaar
SWEET LIME PICKLE

This is a sweet and sour pickle. It tastes good with chappatis and any stuffed paranthas.

12 limes	2 tablespoons salt
1 teaspoon red chilli powder	1 teaspoon garam masala powder
1 teaspoon turmeric powder	6 tablespoons jaggery or brown sugar

Wash the limes and pat them dry with a cloth. Mix all the ingredients in a bowl. Cut the limes into 8 pieces each, and put them in a glass jar. Pour all the mixed ingredients over the limes. Shake the bottle and mix well. Tie a muslin cloth on top of the jar and keep the jar on the window in the kitchen. It will be ready to eat in 15 days time. Shake it daily.

Nimboo Masala Achaar
LEMON SPICY PICKLE

Make this when the lemons are in season. It tastes good with almost anything. Eat it either with puris or chappati, rice, snacks and upma.

12 small lemons	2 tablespoons salt
1 tablespoon garam masala powder	1 teaspoon turmeric powder
1 tablespoon red chilli powder	1 tablespoon ginger root, sliced
6 green chillies, sliced	

Wash and dry the lemons with a cloth. Cut the lemons in 8 pieces. Put the lemons in a tall glass jar along with all the ingredients. Shake the bottle. Tie a muslin cloth on top of the jar and keep on the kitchen window for 15 days. Shake daily.

Achaar

Mirchi Waala Aam ka Achaar
HOT MANGO PICKLE

This is a hot mango pickle made when the green mangoes are in season.

12 green mangoes	$\frac{1}{2}$ cup salt
1 cup oil	1 tablespoon mustard seeds, crushed
1 teaspoon cumin seeds, crushed	12 dried red chillies, coarsely crushed
1 tablespoon turmeric powder	2 cups of oil

Wash the mangoes and dry them with a cloth. Cut the mangoes into 4 pieces but do not separate them at the bottom. Fill each mango with salt, and keep in a glass jar. Tie a muslin cloth over the mouth of the jar and keep in the sun for 3 days. Shake it daily.

Heat 1 cup of oil and remove from the flame. Add all the spices and stir for a minute, cool completely and keep aside. When the spices in the oil are completely cold, fill in the mangoes with the spices. Take another clean jar and put the mangoes upright in it.

Heat the other cup of oil and the drained salt water and cook for about 5 minutes. Cool completely. Pour over the mangoes. See that the mangoes are completely drowned and soaked in the oil. Close again with a muslin cloth so that the pickle can breathe. Keep on the windowsill for about 15 days, so that it gets softer. Do not use any metal spoon to mix the pickle. Always use a wooden spoon for the pickle, or it will get mouldy and rancid.

Achaar

Pyaaz ka Achaar
ONION PICKLE

This is a north Indian pickle. It tastes delicious with dal and rice.

20 button onions (small), peeled
1 cup vinegar
1 teaspoon red chilli powder
1 teaspoon cumin seeds, crushed
1 teaspoon salt
1 teaspoon salt
1 cup jaggery or brown sugar
1 teaspoon garam masala powder
6 cloves of garlic, crushed

Put the whole onions in a glass bowl and add salt. Mix. Put them in a jar and tie a muslin cloth and put in the sun for 2 days. Shake daily.

Open the jar and drain the onions. Place them on a kitchen towel for about 2 hours.

Put vinegar in a deep pan, add jaggery, all the spices and salt; and boil for about 10 minutes.

Add the onions and cook for about 5-10 minutes. Take off from the stove. Cool completely overnight. Put in a jar with a muslin cloth tied on top of the jar. Put on the windowsill for a week, but shake it daily. It would be ready to eat after 7-10 days.

Achaar

Ande ka Achaar
EGG PICKLE

This pickle does not have a very long shelf-life, and so should be consumed soon. It tastes good with bread or rice.

¼ cup oil
1 green chilli, chopped
4 tablespoons grated coconut
1 teaspoon sugar
1 teaspoon red chill powder
2 tablespoons lemon juice
1 teaspoon cumin seeds
6 cloves of garlic
Salt to taste
1 teaspoon turmeric powder
1 teaspoon mustard seeds powder
6 eggs, hard boiled

Heat the oil in a pan. Add the cumin seed, green chilli and garlic. Stir fry for a minute then add the coconut and fry for another 5 minutes. Add the salt and all the other ingredients except the eggs. Stir fry another 2 minutes.

Cut the eggs into halves and put them in a dish. Pour the cooked spices over the eggs and mix gently with a spoon. Serve for lunch or dinner.

Serves: 6

Amrud ki Cheese
GUAVA CHEESE

2 cups guavas, peeled, seeded, chopped
2 cups sugar
1 teaspoon citric acid
A few drops red colour
2 tablespoons butter
Salt to taste
½ cup water

Put the guavas in a pan with butter and sugar. Simmer on a slow fire until it starts to harden. Add the salt, citric acid, water and the red colour. Simmer once again. When it thickens remove from the flame. Pour this guava cheese onto a greased cookie tray. Spread evenly and cool. Cut into squares. Wrap each one in butter paper and keep in fridge.

Papita ka Achaar
PAPAYA PICKLE

One can pickle, make jams, pies, vegetable curries, etc. with this innovative fruit!

1 large raw green papaya	4 cups water
2 cups oil	1/4 teaspoon asafoetida
6 cloves of garlic, crushed	1 teaspoon cumin seeds
1 teaspoon aniseeds	1 teaspoon turmeric powder
1 tablespoon ginger root, sliced	1 teaspoon red chilli powder
2 teaspoons salt	

Peel the papaya and boil it in water. When cooked, drain. Put on a cookie sheet and dry it completely in the sun all day.

Heat oil in a pan. Add the asafoetida, garlic, cumin, aniseeds, turmeric and ginger root and stir fry for about a minute. Take the pan off the flame and cool.

Add the chilli powder, salt and the boiled papaya in the oil. Keep overnight in the pan. Cover with a muslin cloth. Next morning put into a jar. Can be stored in the refrigerator.

Meethe Pakwaan
—Sweet Dishes—

Meethe Pakwaan

In Hindi, we call sweets — 'Mithai'. All Indians enjoy festivals and happy occasions with sweets.

There are many types of sweets in India. Most sweets have a milk and sugar base. Some sweets can also be frozen. Following are some common and some uncommon mithai recipes.

Kheer

Apple halwa

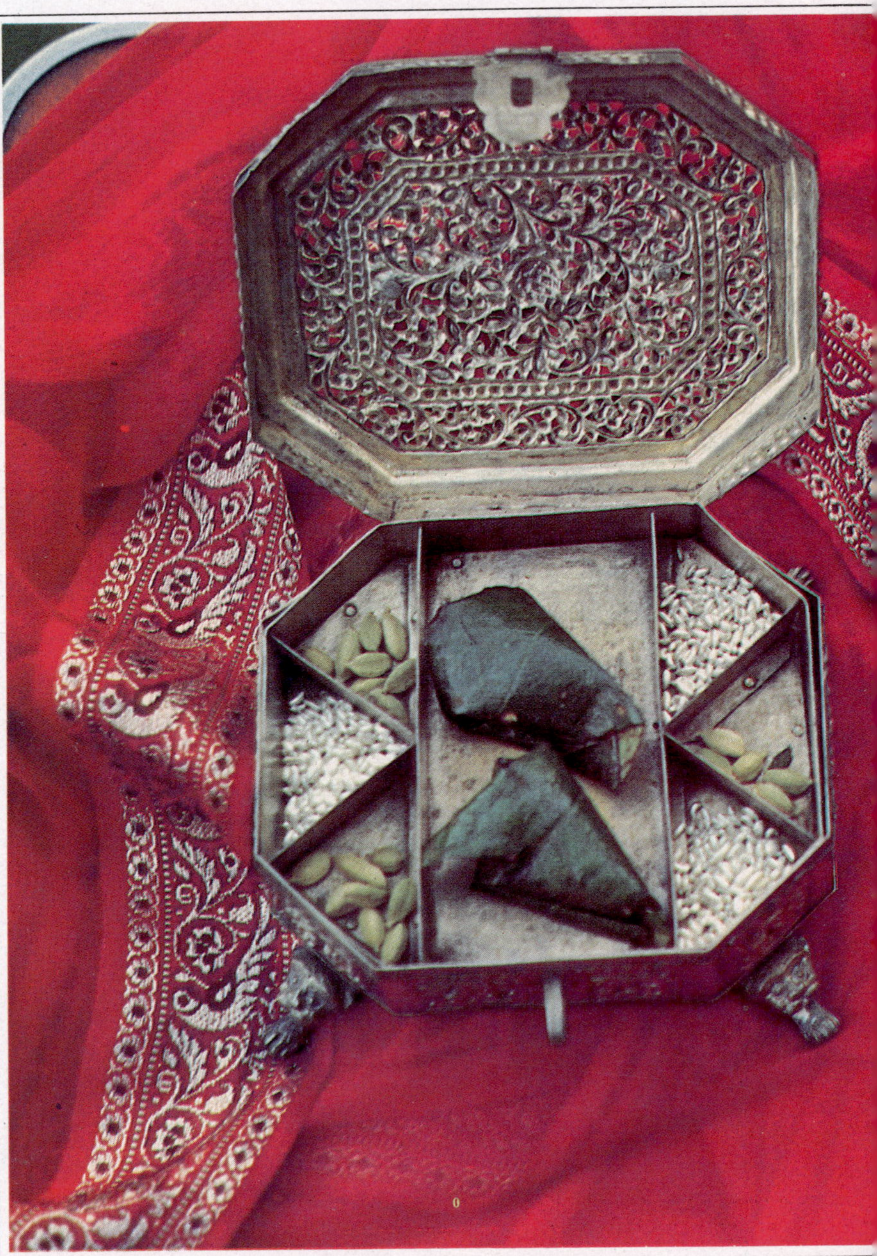

Gulab Jamun

'Paan Daan' with pan, supari and elaichi, sonf etc.

Pakoras with chutney & coffee

Idli, sambhar & chutney

Meethe Pakwaan

Badaam ka Halwa
ALMOND PUDDING

This pudding is very rich in calories but is highly nutritious. It is also eaten in India for good eyesight and sharp memory and usually at weddings.

1 cup sugar	1 cup water
1 cup almonds, soaked and peeled	1 cup ghee
A few drops of 'Kewra' or rose essence	1 teaspoon cardamom powder
1 chaandi varak (silver leaf) optional	

Make a syrup with sugar and water in a pan. Cook it until it becomes a one-thread consistency by pressing a bit of the syrup between your thumb and index finger. If the syrup forms one unbroken string in between your finger and thumb, then it is ready. It is called 'ek taar ki chashni' (one thread syrup). Keep the syrup aside.

Grind the almonds to a fine paste. Heat ghee in a wok and fry the almond paste until it becomes creamy in colour. Add the sugar syrup. Stir it constantly. Cook until the ghee separates from the almonds. Be careful not to burn it.

When ready pour into a greased 'thaali' or plate. Even it out and sprinkle the cardamom powder and put the chaandi varak on top. When cool cut into squares or diamond shapes.

Serves: 6

Meethe Pakwaan

Gajjar ka Halwa
CARROT PUDDING

This halwa is made during the carrot season mostly in North India. One can smell the aroma for miles. It is healthy, rich in carotene and vitamins and recommended for a good eye sight!

3 cups carrots, peeled and grated
$1^1/_2$ cups sugar
1 teaspoon cardamom powder
1 tablespoon almonds, sliced
1 'chaandi varak' (silver leaf) optional

$1^1/_2$ cups milk
$1/_2$ cup ghee
1 tablespoon raisins
1 tablespoon pistachios, sliced

Put the carrots in a large saucepan with milk. Cook them until the carrots are tender. Then add the sugar and keep on cooking on a medium heat. Cook for at least half an hour until it thickens. Add the ghee and keep on stirring for another 20 minutes. Then add the cardamom and raisins. Mix well. Remove from the flame and transfer to a serving dish. Flatten it out with a spoon and sprinkle the nuts on top. Press a 'chaandi varak' on top. Serve hot or cold.

Serves: 6

Meethe Pakwaan

Chana ki Dal ka Halwa
CHICKPEA DAL PUDDING

This is a rich, nutty pudding. It is good to serve after a dinner party.

1 cup chana dal	1 1/2 cups water
1/2 cup ghee	2 tablespoons almonds
1 tablespoon cashewnuts	1/2 cup jaggery or brown sugar

For garnish (optional)

12 almonds sliced 12 pistachios, sliced
6 green cardamoms, seeded, crushed

Boil the chana dal in water until tender. Drain and grind coarsely. Heat ghee in a wok and fry the almonds and cashewnuts. Take them out and chop them. Reheat the ghee and add the ground chana dal. Keep on cooking until the ghee separates. This process will take about 25-30 minutes.

Add the jaggery to the chana dal and cook until the mixture leaves the sides of the pan. Add the chopped fried nuts and mix well.

Turn over on a serving platter. Garnish with sliced almonds and pistachios and cardamom and serve hot.

Serves: 6

Meethe Pakwaan

Mung ki Dal ka Halwa
MUNG DAL PUDDING

This is a special dish from Rajasthan. It is rich, heavy and very filling. Tastes best when served hot.

1 cup yellow split mung beans
½ cup ghee
1 cup sugar
For garnish (optional)
10 almonds, sliced
10 green cardamoms, seeded, crushed

2 cups, water
2 cups milk
1 teaspoon saffron

10 cashewnuts, sliced

Soak the dal overnight in water. Drain. Grind to a fine paste.

Heat the ghee in a wok and fry the ground dal. Keep on stirring on a very low flame, until it turns brown. Meanwhile, boil the milk with sugar and saffron on a separate burner for 10 minutes. When the dal starts to get brown, add the hot milk. Keep on stirring all the time. It should not stick to the wok. Keep stirring until all the milk dries up and the ghee becomes visible over the 'halwa'. It is a tedious task but worth it.

Now put the 'halwa' on a silver platter and sprinkle the almonds, cashewnuts and crushed cardamoms on top. Serve hot.

Serve: 6

Meethe Pakwaan

Matar ki Barfi
PEA TOFFEE

1 cup green peas	2 cups water
1 teaspoon sugar	2 tablespoons ghee
1 cup 'khoa' (see recipe)	$\frac{1}{2}$ cup sugar, ground
1 teaspoon cardamom powder	1 teaspoon almonds, sliced
1 teaspoon pistachios, sliced	1 chaandi varak (silver leaf) optional

Boil peas in water, add sugar. When cooked drain and grind into a smooth paste.

Heat the ghee and fry the pea paste for about 5 minutes. Grate the 'khoa' and mix with the peas. Cook until the 'khoa' becomes soft. Mix the sugar and cardamom powder and cook for about 5-10 minutes more. Pour on a greased plate and press firmly.

Sprinkle the nuts on top and press them in with the back of a bowl. Put the 'chaandi varak'.

When set, cut into squares.

Serves: 6

Meethe Pakwaan

Aam ki Barfi
MANGO TOFFEE

This can be made during the mango season. It is very tasty and can be frozen.

½ cup ghee 1 cup khoa
½ cup milk
½ cup almonds, soaked, peeled and ground
4 cups ripe mangoes, peeled and chopped

For the syrup
2 cups sugar 1 ½ cups water
6 green cardamoms, seeded, crushed

Heat ghee in a wok. Add 'khoa' and roast it well. Keep on stirring until it becomes a nice brown colour. Add the almonds and mix. Keep on stirring.

Mix mangoes and blend in the blender. Strain. Add the mango juice to the wok and cook, stirring constantly.

Prepare the sugar syrup meanwhile on another burner. Add the cardamom to the syrup. Cook the syrup until it thickens and becomes a 3 string syrup (cook one thread sugar syrup for a few minutes more).

Pour the sugar syrup to the contents in the wok and stir thoroughly until the mixture forms one thick mass. Pour it on a greased 'thaali' or cookie tray and leave until set.

Cut into squares.

Serves: 6

Meethe Pakwaan

Aaloo ki Barfi
POTATO TOFFEE

This is a good substitute for days when you are fasting.

2 cups potatoes, peeled and mashed	1 cup 'khoa'
1/2 cup ghee	

For the syrup

2 cups sugar	1 1/2 cup water
Few drops rose or vanilla essence	Few crushed cardamoms

For garnish

12 almonds, sliced
12 pistachios, sliced

Put the mashed potatoes in a bowl and mix with the 'khoa'. Heat the ghee in a wok and roast potato and khoa mixture in the wok until golden brown. Keep aside. Make a syrup with sugar, water, rose essence and cardamoms. Cook the syrup until it reduces to one third of its consistency.

Mix the syrup into the potato and 'khoa' mixture. Stir briskly until it starts solidifying. Quickly pour it onto a greased cookie sheet and sprinkle the nuts over it. Press firmly on top so that the nuts get embedded on top of the aaloo barfi. Cut into square shapes about 2 inches in size.

Serves: 6

Meethe Pakwaan

Khopre ki Barfi
COCONUT TOFFEE

This is a very popular sweet dish all over India. It is made in various colours and is also commercially sold.

1 cup fresh coconut, grated
2 cups sugar
1 tablespoon ghee

2 teaspoons milk (for grinding)
A few drops yellow or green colour

Grind the grated coconut into a smooth paste in the blender with milk.

Put milk in a heavy pan and add the sugar and coconut paste. Cook on a slow flame stirring constantly for almost 45 minutes, until it solidifies. Add the colouring and the ghee. Keep on stirring for about 10 more minutes. Pour onto a greased cookie sheet. When it is cool, cut into diamond shapes.

Serves: 6

Meethe Pakwaan

Gulab Jamun
FRIED MILK BALLS IN ROSE SYRUP

These are soft spongy dark reddish 'brown juicy balls', as the famous Japanese actress Yoko Tani described them.

2 cups milk powder
4 tablespoons self raising flour
1 cup ghee or corn oil, for frying
For the syrup
2 cups sugar
A few drops rose essence
6 crushed green cardamoms with skins on

2 tablespoons butter
$1/2$ cup cold, milk, (approx.)

3 cups water
A pinch of saffron

Knead the milk powder, butter, flour with a little milk into a soft dough. Make into small balls the size of a large marble.

Heat the ghee in a wok and gently fry a few balls at a time on a very low flame. Keep on turning them until they turn a dark reddish brown in colour.

Meanwhile, make a syrup with sugar, and water, until it thickens in about 20 minutes. Add the rose essence, saffron and cardamoms in the syrup.

Drop the fried milk balls into the syrup. Serve them hot or cold.

Yields: 20

Meethe Pakwaan

Naariyal aur Chocolate ke Laddu
COCONUT AND CHOCOLATE BALLS

- 2 cups coconut, grated
- 1 teaspoon chocolate powder
- 1 tablespoon cashewnuts, chopped
- 4 tablespoons desiccated coconut
- ½ tin of condensed milk
- 1 teaspoon cardamom powder
- 1 tablespoon raisins

Make a dough with the coconut, condensed milk, chocolate powder, cardamom, cashewnuts and raisins. Make into round balls.
Put the desiccated coconut on a plate and roll each laddu in the coconut.
Put them on a serving platter.

Serves: 6

Churma Laadu
MASHED SWEET CHAPATTI BALLS

This is a typical dish from Rajasthan. This dish is very popular in the villages, where people have to carry a packed cold lunch. This is made from chappatis, sugar and ghee.

- 1 ½ cups whole wheat flour
- ⅓ cup water (approx.)
- 1 cup ground sugar (boora)
- 2 tablespoons ghee
- 1 cup ghee, for frying

Make a soft dough with the flour, ghee and water. Divide the dough into 6 balls. Flatten them with your palms. Heat the ghee in a wok. Deep fry the flattened dough. Grind the fried dough discs into a fine powder, in the coffee grinder. Again put the ground dough discs in a wok and gently warm it. Mix the sugar when warm and form into 'laadus' (balls) with your right hand. Do it quickly before they turn cold. As they cool they will get firm. It is served as a triple combination of churma, dal, 'baati'.

Serves: 6

Meethe Pakwaan

Khoa ki Gujiya
SWEET MILK PASTRY

This dish is made specially on festivals like 'Holi' and 'Diwali'. These can be kept upto 15-20 days even without refrigeration.

1 cup khoa
1 tablespoon raisins
1 teaspoon cardamom powder
2 tablespoons ghee, for frying

$1/2$ cup semolina
1 tablespoon desiccated coconut
1 teaspoon almonds, chopped

For the pastry shell
2 cups self raising flour, seived
1 teaspoon baking powder
2 cups ghee or oil, for frying

2 tablespoons ghee, melted
$1/2$ cup water (approx.) for kneading

Put the khoa and semolina in a bowl and mix together. Add the raisins, coconut, cardamom and almonds into the khoa mixture. Heat ghee in a wok and gently roast this khoa mixture for a few minutes until it turns golden brown. Keep aside.

Make a soft dough with the flour, ghee, baking powder and water. Divide the dough into 20 equal balls.

Roll each dough ball into a flat disc, about 3 inches in diametre. Place a tablespoonful of the khoa mixture on the disc. Close the disc into half, by sealing the edges with water (use a brush or your tips dipped in water). Close firmly and make a pattern with the back of a fork, pressing the semi-circular disc on the outer edges. Make all in the similar way. Cut the crooked edges with a pastry cutter for a better look!

Heat ghee in a large wok, fry 4 or 5 gujiyas at a time on a slow flame. When a pale biscuit brown appears on both sides, remove. Drain on a paper towel. Cool completely and store in an airtight box.

Yields: 20

Meethe Pakwaan

Elaichi Kheer
CARDAMOM RICE PUDDING

This is a delicious rice and milk pudding and you can serve it hot or cold.

6 cups of milk	1 cup of rice
2 cups sugar	1 tablespoon cardamom powder
1 teaspoon rose essence	A pinch of saffron
2 tablespoon raisins	

For garnishing

1 tablespoon almonds, sliced	1 tablespoon pistachios, sliced

Boil the milk in a heavy bottom saucepan. Add the rice after about 15 minutes. Then add the sugar and cook until the milk and rice thickens and becomes half the quantity. Add the flavourings. Pour into a glass dish. Garnish on top with slivered almonds and pistachios.

Serves: 6

Samaapt
—The End—

Offer betel leaf (Paan) served on a block of ice, with rose petals over the ice blocks. Offer flavoured betel nuts, toasted anise seeds or broken rock candy at the end of each curry meal.

Glossary

English	Hindi	English	Hindi
Allspice	Kabab cheeni	Almonds	Badaam
Aniseed	Saunf	Apple	Seb
Asafoetida	Heeng	Aubergine	Baingan
Bay leaf	Tej patta	Banana	Kela
Beetroot	Chukandar	Bell pepper	Simla mirch
Bengal gram	Chana dal	Betel leaf	Paan
Bitter gourd	Karela	Black gram	Urad dal
Black pepper	Kaali mirch	Black salt	Kaala namak
Bowl	Katori	Butter	Makkhan
Buttermilk	Chaach	Bread	Roti, Naan
Betel Nut	Supari	Brinjal	Baingan
Cabbage	Bund gobhi	Cauliflower	Gobhi
Cardamoms	Elaichi	Carrots	Gajjar
Cashewnuts	Kaaju	Carom seeds	Ajwain
Cereals	Anaaj	Cheese	Paneer
Cinnamon	Dalcheeni	Cocoyam or colocasia	Arbi
Chilli	Mirchi		
Cumin	Zeera or jeera	Cloves	Laung
Curds (Yogurt)	Dahi	Coconut	Nariyal
Garlic	Lahsun	Cucumber	Kakari (kheera)
Ginger root	Adrak	Garbanzo	Chhola
Grapes	Angoor	Garnish	Sajawat
Gram flour	Besan *(Chickpea)*	Gravy	Shorva or rasa
Groundnut	Mungphali	Green chilli	Hari mirch
Green mango	Kairee	Guava	Amrood
Herbs	Hara masala	Honey	Shehad
Jack fruit	Kathal	Horse raddish	Muli
Jaggery	Gur	Kewra essence	Kewra jal
Lemon	Neembu	Lentils (Pulses)	Dals
Lettuce	Salaad	Lime	Neembu
Mace	Javitri	Maize	Makka or Bhuttaa
Mango	Aam	Milk	Dudh

English	Hindi	English	Hindi
Millet	Baajra	Mint	Podina
Mould	Sancha	Mushroom	Guchhi
Mustard seed	Rai or Sarson	Musk melon	Kharbooza
Nutmeg	Jaiphal	Okra	Bhindi
Oil	Tel	Olive	Jetoon or zetun
Onion	Pyaaz	Onion seed	Mangrail or Kalonji
Oranges	Narangi or Santra	Oven	Chulha
Pastry board	Chakla	Pears	Nashpaati
Peanut	Mungphali	Peas (green)	Matar
Pepper	Kaali mirch	Pineapple	Annanas
Pistachios	Pista	Papaya	Papita
Plum	Aloo bukhaara	Poppy seeds	Khus Khus
Potato	Aaloo	Pulses	Dal
Pumpkin	Kaddu	Pomegranate seeds	Anaardaana
Radish	Mooli		
Red Chilli	Laal mirch	Raisins	Kishmish
Rice (raw)	Chaawal	Refined flour	Maida
Rice flakes	Poha	Rice (cooked)	Chaawal, Pullao or Bhaat
Rice Pancakes	Dosa		
Saffron	Kesar or Zaffraan	Sago	Sabudaana
Salt	Namak	Semolina	Sooji
Sesame seeds	Til	Solidified milk	Khoa
Soup	Shorba or shorva	Spices	Masala
Spinach	Paalak	Sugar	Cheeni
Syrup	Chashni	Silver leaf	Chaandi varak
Seeds	Beej	Sweets	Mithai
Tamarind	Imli	Tomato	Tamatar
Turnip	Shaljam	Vegetable	Sabzi or Tarkaari
Vermicelli	Sevian, Faluda	Vinegar	Sirka
Walnut	Akhrot	Water	Paani
Water melon	Tarbuz	Wheat flour	Aataa
Whole wheat	Gehun	Whole wheat bread	Chappati
Whole wheat fried bread	Poori		
Yogurt shake	Lassi	White Pumpkin (Zuchini)	Lauki
Yolk (egg)	Zurdee		